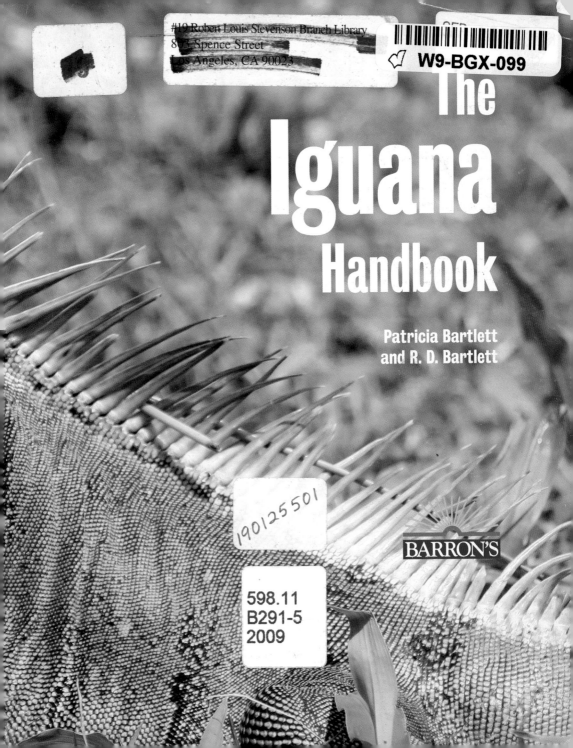

The Iguana Handbook

Patricia Bartlett and R. D. Bartlett

BARRON'S

Acknowledgments

We'd like to thank the researchers, scientists and hobbyists who have dedicated so much of their lives and resources to the green iguana. Because of them, the care of captive iguanas has changed for the better, and because they've brought their findings to the countries concerned, conservation methods are being implemented for these lizards.

We especially wish to acknowledge Fredric Frye, Douglas Mader, and Susan Donoghue; Walter Meshaka, Billy Griswold, Collette Adams, Tom Van Devender, Wayne Van Devender, and Abby and the late George Heit; Alice Clark, Pam Krause, and Dan Scolaro; Rob MacInnes and Mike Stuhlman; Marian Bacon; Travis Knowles; Jonathan Moser; Donna Lindemann; Kathy Russell and Lara Maxwell.

Frank Indiviglio evaluated and commented on the original manuscript; thank you.

We thank our editor, Anthony Regolino, for his sense of what fits and what does not.

©Copyright 2009, 2000 by Barron's Educational Series, Inc.

All rights reserved.
No part of this publication may be reproduced or distributed in any form or by any means without the written permission of the copyright owner.

All inquiries should be addressed to:
Barron's Educational Series, Inc.
250 Wireless Boulevard
Hauppauge, New York 11788
www.barronseduc.com

ISBN-13: 978-0-7641-4141-6
ISBN-10: 0-7641-4141-4

Library of Congress Catalog Card No. 2008053597

Library of Congress Cataloging-in-Publication Data

Bartlett, Patricia Pope, 1949–
    The iguana handbook / Patricia Bartlett, R. D. Bartlett. — 2nd ed.
        p.   cm.
    Includes bibliographical references and index.
    ISBN-13: 978-0-7641-4141-6
    ISBN-10: 0-7641-4141-4
    1. Iguanas as pets. I. Bartlett, Richard D., 1938– . II. Title.

SF459.I38B36   2009
639.3'9542—dc22   2008053597

Printed in China

9 8 7 6 5 4 3 2 1

About the Authors

Patricia Bartlett received her B.S. from Colorado State University and became the editor for an outdoor book publisher in St. Petersburg, Florida. Subsequently, she worked for the science museum in Springfield, Massachusetts, and for the historical museum in Ft. Myers, Florida. She is the author or co-author of fifty books on natural history and historical subjects.

R. D. Bartlett is a herpetologist who has authored many articles and books on reptiles. He lectures extensively and has participated in field studies across North and Latin America. In 1978 he began the Reptilian Breeding and Research Institute (RBRI), a private facility. Since its inception, more than 150 species of reptiles and amphibians have been bred at RBRI, some for the first time in the United States under captive conditions. Successes at the RBRI include several endangered species.

Photo Credits

Joan Balzarini: 63; Gerry Bucsis and Barbara Somerville: 52, 61 (bottom), 62, 111, 119, 135; Cheryl A. Ertlet: 140. All other photos are by R. D. Bartlett.

Cover Photos

Shutterstock: front cover, back cover, inside front cover, inside back cover.

Important Note

While handling iguanas, you may occasionally receive bites, scratches, or tail blows. If your skin is broken, see your physician immediately.

Some terrarium plants may be harmful to the skin or mucous membranes of human beings. If you notice any signs of irritation, wash the area thoroughly. See your physician if the condition persists.

Iguanas may transmit certain infections to humans. Always wash your hands carefully after handling your specimens. Always supervise children who wish to observe your iguanas.

Contents

Preface

During the 1990s, giant green iguanas caught the public's fancy as pets, and enormous numbers of them—largely wild caught—were imported into the United States from South America. (In 1997 alone, the count was more than 973,000.) The vast majority of them died, due to bad diets and poor housing. Those that somehow survived presented another problem. It's like the proverbial 400-pound gorilla, with a twist. What does one do with a five-foot-long lizard with a mean tail? Very few iguana owners knew what to do with an adult iguana.

Since then, giant green iguanas are farm-raised in South America and far fewer come into the United States. (The exact number is elusive because no U.S. agency is required to collect numbers of captive bred iguanas brought into the United States.) But young iguanas are still as appealing as they were 20 years ago, and their new owners are still faced with the same question: what happens when that baby iguana outgrows its saucy baby appearance? That's why we've written this book, to help the iguana owner, new or experienced, enjoy his or her iguana throughout its 20-year or more life span, and to help make captivity a nonstressful life for all those owners and their iguanas.

Before you decide you really would like an iguana, make a few phone calls first. Municipalities are looking at iguana possession and they don't like the picture. New York City led the way in 1999 by outlawing the keeping of giant green iguanas and "other dangerous" creatures such as pythons and ferrets. The aim of the law was to prevent people from buying these nondomesticated animals on an impulse and then dumping the animal when they find the care was more than they expected and the animal's behavior wasn't what they thought it would be. There's not much of a resale market for adult, untamed iguanas, pythons, or ferrets. They're often dropped off at already overcrowded shelters or summarily discarded. In gentle climates, the discarded iguanas survive, breed, and become established.

Iguanas are not for everyone, nor should they be. But for some of us, they provide a fascinating window into a world where beauty, instinct, and nature meet.

Chapter One
The Green Iguana

There's no place like home,
expanded home . . .

The green iguana is a large tree-dwelling lizard found from southern Mexico to northern South America. In the last 30 years, this lizard has been in the curious position of becoming less common in its original range, while becoming established in at least four new areas across the world. It has been introduced, either accidentally or on purpose, into the Hawaiian Islands, Texas, and Florida. (Planned conservation efforts for Hawaii have been slated to remove the green iguana from all of the Hawaiian islands.) It has also, in some cases, apparently through deliberate efforts, been established on a few of the islands of the Lesser Antilles.

The green iguana is also a beautiful lizard. The big adults, resplendent in their fringed crests, green to orange coloring, massive dewlaps, and haughty demeanor, are an impressive sight. But it is the baby iguanas, those Kool-Aid lime-green-colored hatchlings with the milk chocolate sidebars and insouciant toffee-colored eyes, that captured the fancy of millions of hobbyists in the 1990s and still continue to due so.

Any hobbyist who has been in a pet store in the past ten years knows about baby green iguanas. If a pet store sells reptiles, chances are that a brilliantly lit tank, with a few of these bright green, bright-eyed lizards, forms the focal point of the reptile department. But iguanas have not always been common pets, nor are they ideal pets.

Description

The green iguana is a big lizard—hence the new name "giant green iguana"—that is adept at running, climbing, and swimming, all useful skills for a lizard long regarded as a human food source in its native land.

Bygone Days

I (RDB) can remember the first ad I ever saw for the great green iguana as a pet. I was in junior high school, and the listing was in a catalog issued by the long-defunct Quivira Specialties Company of Topeka,

A New Population

Sometimes, unexpected factors can extend the range of iguanas. In October 1995, 15 green iguanas became marooned on a thatch of waterlogged trees that eventually landed on the island of Anguilla. Using currents and recent storm patterns as guides, researchers felt the lizards had originated from Guadalupe, some 200 miles (320 km) away. (The previous month, September, had seen two hurricanes, Luis and Marilyn, move through the Caribbean.) At least 15 iguanas crept off the thatch once it landed, but there may have been more. All showed signs of their prolonged sea journey, appearing weak and dehydrated, but they all dispersed into the brush on Anguilla. Six months later, in March 1996, researchers on Anguilla found a pregnant female green iguana. Not only were those 15 iguanas the first green iguanas on the island, but the pregnant female has special significance. This establishing of a reproductive population of a species new to the island lends credibility to the long-held theory that new animals can be established from one island to another by traveling on natural rafts.

Kansas. They advertised their free catalogs in the classified sections of the fishing and hunting magazines. I sent away for a catalog, entranced by the come-on of 85-cent horned lizards and the dizzying visions of other wonderful animals I could buy.

When the catalog came, the first reptile I noticed was the green iguana. I was so excited about the prospect of owning an iguana that I could hardly sleep. Of course, I had to gather the needed money together first (about $5.00, including postage), something that was not always easy for me to do when my allowance covered only school lunches, at 25 cents each. But by the time I gathered the money, the baby iguana lost out to the allure of a baby red-tailed boa that was selling for the same price.

It was not until a few years later when a teacher, a herper like myself, walked into the classroom with a baby great green iguana perched jauntily on his shoulder that I finally came face to face with this lizard. In all honesty, at first I paid more attention to the lizard than the person who carried it in. The teacher was E. Gordon (Gordy) Johnston, who, despite our age difference, quickly became my friend, mentor, and nearly constant herping companion. I had by then lost some interest in my boa, so an exchange was struck, the result being that Gordy became the proud possessor of a boa and I of the iguana.

This wonderful pet lizard ate every inappropriate kind of food I offered it, and it grew despite all of my erroneous iguana-diet beliefs. However, a year or so later, the lizard died from a malady I know now to be metabolic bone disease (MBD), but that was then called rickets. I was devas-

Baby iguanas are shipped when only a few weeks old and perhaps just ten inches in length.

tated, and thoroughly perplexed. It was obvious to me that I had done something wrong, but what was that something?

In those days—the 1940s—it was as easy, or as difficult, to get a baby iguana as it was a boa or an Indian python. All were inexpensive, all were periodically available in some numbers, but there were few animal importers. Reptiles were available primarily through only a handful of dealers; very few pet stores sold reptiles—after all, who would actually *buy* a reptile? Hobbyists, myself included, knew comparatively little about the regimen of husbandry needed—this was particularly so for the green iguana.

Early Importing

It was not until the late 1950s and early 1960s that iguana imports began to increase. By then baby iguanas were collected from the wild, and there were enough buyers to make reptile exporters sit up and take notice. Because we still knew

little about the actual dietary needs of the lizards, there were no care booklets of any sort. Iguana longevity was dismal. Both sellers and hobbyists tended to consider iguanas a hard-to-keep-alive but easily replaced pet lizard. There were, however, a few iguanas that lived to maturity, more despite our efforts than because of them. Anyone who had the magic touch needed to raise one of these lacertilian giants became the envy of the many who had failed. Florence Guttierez, a Cuban-born veterinarian who relocated to Miami in the early 1960s, was one of these magicians. Her iguanas, Sunny and Brigette, went everywhere with her, often riding on the dashboard of her car. Florence believed in a varied diet, including an occasional orchid blossom.

Little changed in the late sixties, the seventies, or the early eighties. Baby iguanas were imported in increasing numbers, baby iguanas were sold in increasing numbers, and baby iguanas succumbed in increasing numbers because of our continuing misconceptions about the dietary and caging needs of these lizards.

Iguanas in the Eighties— An Age of Revelation

In 1982 Gordon M. Burghardt and A. Stanley Rand, as editors, gathered together the pertinent iguana research of 31 contributing scientists and published *Iguanas of the World, Their Behavior, Ecology, and Conservation*. Field observations and lab research brought to light information about iguanas that pinpointed many areas where we had been wrong. The book has become a classic in iguana research.

Beginning about the same time, and continuing until today, veterinarians, professional herpetologists, and dietary researchers paid serious attention to the dietary needs of the great green iguana. Pet food manufacturers were quick to realize the potential of how much food a million iguana mouths a year could consume, and began their own research projects.

Prominent among these veterinarian/researchers were Drs. Frederic L. Frye, Susan Donaghue, Douglas Mader, and Patrick Morris. Thanks to the research of these folks, and of others, we were finally able to determine that our big dietary lapse was in treating the great green iguana as we did other large lizards, as an insectivore and a carnivore, with perhaps a little vegetation thrown in for good measure. Admittedly, we had been guided in part by the appetites of the iguanas themselves. Iguanas eagerly chow down crickets, mealworms, and mice. The bigger lizards would literally run across the cage to get at such high-fat and unnatural food items. Unfortunately, we were killing the lizards with indulgence when we should have been providing them with a base diet of greens instead (no parallel with human diets is intended).

Differences of Opinion

Typical of scientists and researchers, there still are some differences of opinion. Some researchers have gone so far as to say that any dietary animal protein may harm an iguana, and that wild iguanas do not consume animal protein, whether it is invertebrate or vertebrate. After having watched wild iguanas in Colombia, in Mexico, and in Miami, Florida eagerly crunch down grasshoppers, katydids, and caterpillars they happen across, we do not subscribe to this concept of full exclusivity of diet. But we do recognize that when fed a good, healthy, vegetable diet, the life span of a captive green iguana can be measured in years—actually in decades—rather than months, and their overall health can best be described as exuberant.

Iguanas Today

Great green iguanas became so popular a pet trade species that they began to be farmed farmed in vast

Offered a diet of mixed greens, young iguanas grow quickly. These iguanas are about 14 months old, and about a third of their adult size.

quantities in the Latin American countries of their origin. Adult females are bred with adult males. The resultant eggs are incubated and the hatchlings sold. Entire acres were cleared and planted with fast-growing foods for the adults. Shade cloth and wire mesh enclosures were erected to house the adults, and sandy areas for nest-digging were placed in the females' enclosures. Cleared areas were scraped around the "compounds" so they could be protected from predators. The farming of iguanas assures the pet trade that baby iguanas will be available for more months of the year, and the drain on wild populations is considerably lessened.

Your Long-term Commitment

So, the question for you, the hobbyist, is not how long you can keep your baby iguana alive, but whether you are prepared to take on this long-term commitment. This is a pet that may live longer than a dog or cat, may attain a length of more than 6 feet (1.8 m) and need a cage the size of a room at adulthood, that needs a specific diet and dietary supplements, and that just might become intractable during its breeding season or at other times (see the section on Thwarting Iguana Aggression, pages 126–128). You must also be aware that it is almost impossible to find a new home for a large iguana that has for one reason or another outgrown its welcome. Zoos don't want them. Nature centers usually exhibit only local wildlife, and those that accept out-of-area animals already have far too many iguanas. Other hobbyists who might have once wanted a large iguana are raising their own. Simply turning these cold-sensitive lizards loose is morally wrong and is illegal as well.

Although this black spiny tail was photographed in Costa Rica, the lizard has become established in southern Florida.

In most cases, the only option becomes euthanasia. The lizard simply does not deserve that fate. Always remember that it was your choice, not the iguana's, that brought it into your family. From the moment of acquisition, your iguana deserves the very best that you are able to provide throughout its life.

Iguanas in the United States

Today, in the United States, including Hawaii, there are six species of iguanid lizards. Two species, the desert iguana and the northern chuckwalla, are native to our desert Southwest, and are found in suitable habitats in Arizona, California, Nevada, and Utah. Four, the great green iguana and three species of spiny-tailed iguanas, are intro-duced species, and may be encountered in the states of Florida, Texas, Arizona, and Hawaii. (For more on other iguanas, see pages 67–71.)

Green iguanas, desert iguanas, and chuckwallas are easily differentiated from the other iguanid species. Spiny-tails can be another matter entirely; the exact identification of two of the species can be very difficult and may require chromosomal analysis. Additionally, although readily identifiable as to species, the three subspecies of chuckwalla that occur north of the Mexican border can also be difficult to differentiate.

The green iguana and our three spiny-tailed iguanas are large species, the males of all exceeding 3½ feet (106 cm) in nose-to-tail length when adult, although more than half the length is tail. The desert iguana and the chuckwalla are smaller, seldom attaining 15 inches (38 cm) in length.

Where to See Iguanas in the United States

Common name	Scientific name	Where found in the United States
Great green iguana	*Iguana iguana*	Southern Florida, some Hawaiian Islands, southern Texas
Mexican spiny-tailed iguana	*Ctenosaura pectinata*	Southern Florida, southern Texas
Black spiny-tailed iguana	*Ctenosaura similis*	Southern Florida
Sonoran spiny-tailed iguana	*Ctenosaura h. hemilopha*	Southern Arizona
Desert iguana	*Dipsosaurus dorsalis*	Western Arizona, southeastern California, southern Nevada, extreme southwestern Utah
Chuckwalla	*Sauromalus ater*	Utah, Arizona, California

You can see green iguanas along the tributaries of the Amazon or along canals in Miami.

Southern Florida has proven a suitable region for the colonization and long-term reproduction of the great green iguana, the Mexican spiny-tailed iguana, and the black spiny-tailed iguana, much to the dismay of several municipalities. All three are now firmly established residents that will probably persist despite hired "iguana hunters." Two of those three, the great green iguana and the Mexican spiny-tailed iguana, are also known to occur in the Lower Rio Grande Valley of Texas, but their exact status there is not known with certainty. Other than in Brownsville and its immediate environs, and seemingly primarily on the grounds of the Gladys Porter Zoo, the continued existence of the two is probably tenuous at best.

The third species, the Sonoran spiny-tailed iguana, only occurs in Arizona, and in that state, it is thought to be restricted to the grounds of the Arizona-Sonora Desert Museum. It was deliberately released there at least three decades ago, and although having established itself in fair numbers, and continuing to breed yearly, is not known to have expanded its range.

The only iguana in Hawaii is the great green iguana. In conversation, the late Sean McKeown, former supervising herpetologist at the Honolulu Zoo, had informed us that the great green iguana has been present on the island for more than 40 years, but that as far as is known, no ecological damage has been attributed to this large lizard. It seems most common on the island of Oahu, but is known to occur sparingly on a few smaller outlying islands also. Its presence in Hawaii has been attributed to an equable climate nurturing the well-being of escaped and discarded pets.

Great Green Iguanas

In the three states where they now occur, great green iguanas regularly utilize every imaginable habitat except the air and the open sea. They may be seen foraging in tree canopies, hiding beneath canal side debris, thermoregulating warily on

The Sonoran spiny-tailed iguana is native to Sonoran Mexico, where it prefers rocky outcroppings. Or you can find them at the Sonoran Desert Museum in Arizona.

downtown sidewalks, or devouring prized hibiscus in urban backyards. Green iguanas swim in both fresh and saltwater.

Clutches of up to 35 eggs have been found in Florida. Where the soil is soft enough, the female will usually dig an extensive nesting chamber, but some energy-conserving females merely angle their nesting chamber inward beneath surface debris such as discarded plywood, a large rock, or an old mattress. The eggs are then laid, often almost in contact with the cover.

Both males and females are territorial, but males become especially so during the breeding season. They indulge in pushups, rapid head bobs, tail-slapping, and actual skirmishing to rout interloping iguanas. If threatened with capture and not able to escape, adults will slap with the tail. If actually captured, their raking hind feet and enthusiastic biting will quickly open wounds.

The great green iguana has so far been able to tolerate the vagaries of south Florida's weather. Individuals have been sighted further north in the state, but may die during the passage of winter cold fronts. Green iguanas may be so immobilized by cold they literally fall out of trees.

Sonoran Spiny-tailed Iguanas

Range alone will allow you to identify the Sonoran spiny-tailed iguana, *Ctenosaura h. hemilopha*, in the United States. This impressive lizard has 75 to 107 dorsal crest

A photographer gets eye to eye with the black spiny-tail. This lizard lived in a park, and associated people with handouts (yes, this ctenosaur did eat Twinkies).

scales, with the crest being interrupted (decreased radically) above the hind legs for more than 24 scale rows. Each spinose whorl of caudal (tail) scales is separated from the next by a single row of small scales. Look for this up-to-30-inch lizard on sunny days on pathside boulders and on the tops of walls and buildings on the grounds of the Arizona-Sonora Desert Museum in Tucson, Arizona. Hatchlings are green, banded with dark pigment. Adults are gray, banded with black.

Mexican and Black Spiny-tailed Iguanas

The Mexican and the black spiny-tailed iguanas are so similar in external appearance that in Dade County, Florida, where the two occur sympatrically, they are almost impossible to differentiate visually. If you're on Key Biscayne, you can guess you're looking at the black spiny-tailed iguana; it is currently the more common on that key. In Dade County, it is probably best to merely call the lizards a species complex, rather than attempt a specific identification. Both species have dorsal crests that may or may not be interrupted above the hind legs, but if so, for fewer than 21 scale rows. It was long thought that the Mexican spiny-tail, *C. pectinata*, had a minimum of three rows of small scales separating each of the large, spinose, caudal whorls from the next, but continuing research is divulging that this external characteristic overlaps that of the black spiny-tail, *C. similis.* As minute as these morphological details may seem, they are distinguishable in the field. DNA studies, on the other hand, may give you absolutely accurate species ID, but you can't use DNA analysis in the field, and it isn't free.

Look for the Mexican spiny-tailed iguana on mainland Dade County, Florida, where it can be seen along the streets and in the ornamental trees of metropolitan Miami. It is also common on Boca Grande Island (Lee County, Florida), where it is now broadly disliked for its appetite, and may be present on other Gulf Coast islands as well. In Texas, this lizard may be seen roaming on the grounds of the zoo in the city of Brownsville.

The two spiny-tails enjoy many of the same behavioral characteristics as the green iguana, but they do not seem to swim as readily. They do deposit from 12 to about 25 eggs in the late spring. Nests may angle beneath man-made or natural surface debris, or be placed in the open. Large, healthy females deposit more and larger eggs than smaller specimens.

Hatchlings of the Mexican spiny-tail are grayish but change to a pale

Young black spiny-tailed iguanas are bright green and look a bit like young green iguanas.

A desert iguana will move into available desert shade once he (or she) warms up.

green within just a few days. With growth they gradually assume the adult coloration of black bars on a tan ground. Hatchlings of the black spiny-tail are also gray when hatched, but soon assume a bright green juvenile coloration.

The adults of both, usually gray, banded with black, become brighter during the breeding season; then the sides of the males are often washed with yellow or orange.

These are alert and wary lizards that know their home territories well. They are often seen basking, head raised well away from the ground, on piles of rubble and building materials. They retire to burrows at night and in inclement weather, and dart to the burrows if frightened during the day.

The Desert Iguana

The desert iguana, *Dipsosaurus dorsalis*, is quietly colored but remarkably pretty. It is often referred to as the "dipso." The range of the desert iguana closely follows that of the creosote bush, which they eat, and virtually parallels that of the chuckwalla. At present, there is but a single nonsubspeciated type recognized. Look for these lizards on hot summer days as they dash to and from the cover of low desert shrubs. They are common along many desert roadways, and may almost always be seen during a summer drive through Organ Pipe National Park near Ajo, Arizona, and in Joshua Tree National Park, near Twentynine Palms, California. Their camouflage colors can render desert iguanas nearly invisible as they bask in the tracery of shadows beneath leafless desert shrubs. Although they tend to be visible when they run, they're too fast to catch. Desert iguanas are primarily terrestrial and are adept at burrowing, but they may clamber into low shrubs as well. When closely threatened, these lizards take off on a dead (often bipedal) run toward their burrow.

The desert iguana is heavy-bodied, but not fat. It has a short head with a rounded snout, stout limbs, and a tapering tail that is about equal in length to that of the head and body. Except for the low vertebral crest, the body scales are small, while those of the tail are large and arranged in prominent whorls. The ground color of the desert iguana is changeable, usually approximating the color of the sand in which it dwells. An overlay of brown or brownish red occurs on the sides. On breeding males this often brightens to a pink or pinkish orange. Light ocelli are present anteriorly, wavy lines posteriorly.

These are true sun worshipers that may be out and active at mid-day when desert temperatures are in the 115 to 120°F (46–48.9°C) range.

In a burrow of their own making, female desert iguanas lay a single clutch of from two to nine eggs in mid-spring to early summer. Incubation seems to take somewhat more than two months.

The Chuckwalla

The chuckwalla, *Sauromalus ater*, is an inhabitant of desert boulder fields and escarpments. The males are by far the larger and more colorful sex. Both sexes are clad in baggy skin that looks like oversized pajamas. They may occasionally attain 15 to 16 inches (38–41 cm) in total length, but are more often about a foot (30 cm) long.

When driving through suitable habitat in such areas as Organ Pipe or Joshua Tree National Parks or Anza Borrego Desert State Park, it is not uncommon on hot, sunny afternoons to see the big lizards sprawled, but attentive, on top of rocks both distant and near. Rest assured, they see you long before you see them. Should you even begin to slow down, the lizards will become more watchful, and by the time you stop for a better look (binoculars help), the chuck will have scuttled in its curious spraddle-legged walk, over the boulder and into a crevice. Once in the far reaches of a crevice, they inflate their bodies to make their removal impossible.

Diet: Besides the buds, blossoms, and some leaves of the creosote bush, chucks consume

The chuckwalla Sauromalus ater *has a scaly shield over its tympanum (eardrum).*

This is an endangered San Esteban Island chuckwalla, Sauromalus varius.

considerable amounts of other vegetation, the flowers, leaves, and seeds of many desert annuals and perennials included. Some insects are also consumed.

Breeding: Chucks are oviparous lizards, the females laying a single clutch consisting of from a few to nearly a dozen large eggs. It is conjectured that many wild females produce their clutches only every second year. Captive females, traditionally better fed and having a somewhat longer annual activity period, may produce annually.

Chuckwallas have a relatively short annual activity period. As would be expected from a large lizard in a temperate climate, they emerge from hibernation rather late in the year—mid- to late-April, depending on temperature—and hibernate again well before the cold weather has truly set in. While up and about, chucks are active only during the warmest part of the day. A body temperature from 99 to 102°F (37.2–38.9°C) seems to be their operating optimum. At that temperature, for such big, heavy lizards, they are active, alert, wary, and even somewhat agile.

Although laws protect the chuckwalla from collection for the pet trade, they are quick to avoid any human contact. Here one peers from a rock crevice where it has taken refuge.

Chapter Two

The Basic Green Iguana

The physical green iguana is a well-adapted package, able to run, swim, climb, eat, mate, and accomplish a number of activities directed toward its survival.

Activities

One of the activities a green iguana does best is—just nothing. Iguanas spend most of their waking hours recumbent on tree limbs, resting and watching. Groups of iguanas in captivity are active for about 45 minutes in the morning and in the afternoon. The remainder of the time, they are inactive, rousing every two to eight minutes to blink, nod, tongue-flick or look around. They are superb energy conservers, a needed skill for an animal that actually gets very little nourishment from the food it consumes.

If you compare an iguana's activities on an energy-use perspective, you'll see that the lizard's activities are directly related to energy conservation. It takes less energy to drop

A green iguana checks for scent trails.

off a tree limb and swim away than it does to stay and defend a tree limb territory. It takes less energy to dig a shallow burrow for egg deposition, or to appropriate another burrow— than it does to dig a deeper burrow, and the list goes on.

Body Features

Not only are iguanas energy-conserving animals, but they are unique in many ways. Let's look at some of the body features that make them well adapted to their environment.

Pores: Like other lizards, iguanas have a series of pores called *femoral pores* along the underside of the hind legs. These are best developed in the males. The pores secrete a waxy gray substance, which contains scenting molecules called pheromones that are used to mark territory. As iguanas crawl along, the femoral pores drag along the surface of the trail and leave a scent trail. The scent trail left by the iguana does not absorb UV rays so it is not visible to the iguana, but it doesn't need to be. This is an *olfactory trail*. The scent dissipates best in humid conditions. In heavily vegetated areas such as the green iguanas' habitat, which is heavily overgrown in comparison to the desert iguanas' habitat, sight is often useful only for a very limited distance. But iguanas need to know where other iguanas, particularly large males, are, without having to see them. They also need to know where the territorial lines have, quite literally, been drawn.

This is the opposite of desert iguanas, where sight is an important factor in locating other desert iguanas. Their femoral secretions absorb UV rays, which makes the trail visible to other desert iguanas. When a desert iguana comes across a scent trail, it can follow the trail by sight without relying on olfactory clues.

Spines

The soft spines along the back-bone help the iguana look larger. They lie along a muscular, erectile crest, which can be contracted to make the spines stand up. The large neck spines seem to be an adaptation to the habitat. Iguanas from desert regions, such as the desert iguanas, have very reduced dorsal spines. Chuckwallas, a group of iguanids that seek refuge between rocks, have no dorsal spines at all. When it is present, the crest is larger and more pronounced in the males than in the females; perceived size is a real factor in territorial disputes. Female iguanas often wear their crest down in digging burrows for egg deposition.

Many green iguanas from Mexico and northern Central America also bear pronounced elongated scales or spines near the tip of the snout. When damaged, through territorial disputes or in banging against caging in captivity, neither the crest nor the nose "spines" fully regenerate.

Note: At one time, these lizards were classified as the now-invalid subspecies, *I. i. rhinolopha*.

Legs and Claws

The legs are long, making for a respectable stride in running as well as agility and speed in climbing. There is a very practical use for the long legs and claws; the claws help in grasping tree trunks and limbs and that long stride translates into a long reach with claws at the end, and a stressed iguana is quick to rake an aggressor with all four feet. The curved shape of the claws is due to the upper layer of keratin growing faster than the lower layer of the claw, causing the claw to curl as it grows.

Tail: The tail of the iguana is its most powerful appendage. Not only does it help in balancing the animal during climbs, but it serves as a rudder and propulsion device while the iguana is swimming. It can also be a formidable weapon. If you try to pick up an alarmed iguana, a stinging blow from its tail will raise a welt on your arm. If your face is too close to the iguana and it strikes you across the face, the impact will bring tears

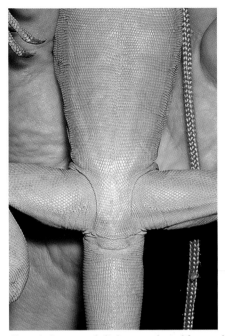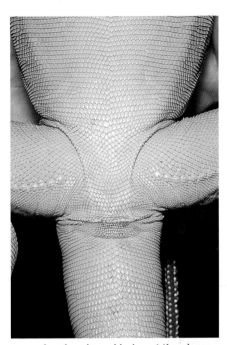

Female iguanas, left, have reduced femoral pores and no hemipenal bulge at the cloaca; males, right, have distinct femoral pores and a hemipenal bulge at the cloaca.

to your eyes. Some researchers feel the blow is forceful enough to deter the advances of potential predators. Losing the tail, or a portion of it, is part of the iguana's defense package. Young iguanas especially have the ability to lose their tail. Called *caudal autotomy*, there's an obvious advantage to being able to leave part of your tail in a predator's grasp while you run off to safety!

Dewlap: All iguanas bear a dewlap, a fold of skin under the throat. Always visible, the dewlap is further distended during courtship and territorial displays; it is larger in the males. It is the males that are more emphatic in their aggressive-defensive displays, but the females also display. In adulthood, the males tend to be larger, have heavier jowls and swollen temporal areas, and are often brighter in overall coloration than females. The colors that develop during the breeding season may be related to the geographic origin of the iguana; some iguanas develop blue- or rose-flushed faces, some develop orange sides, while others may become intensely green with dark side bars.

The dewlap is also used in thermoregulation, being fully distended in the morning as the iguana turns its body sideways to expose the greatest surface area to the sun's

Green iguanas have strong, curved claws on each foot to aid in climbing and in defense.

warmth. The iguana will also darken its body to absorb more heat, and will flatten its body from side to side, in order to present the greatest surface area to the sun for warming.

If the iguana becomes too warm, it will lighten its color and move to a cooler area. There, the surface area of the distended dewlap will help the lizard drop its temperature to a more

The pineal organ is light receptive.

comfortable level. Panting may also be utilized, but this can also be a danger signal. An iguana trapped in the sun or in a cage that's too warm will pant, essentially as a last-ditch effort to cool off. It doesn't have long to cool off; if it cannot cool off, it will die.

Parietal eye: On the crown of the head, between and just a little posterior to the eyes, is a small grayish organ that looks like a modified scale. This is the parietal eye, which is sensitive to light and dark cycles (photoperiod) and thus aids in the timing of the breeding cycle. The parietal eye bears a vestigial lens, a retina, and is part of the endocrine system. This pineal organ, or parietal eye, is a sensory organ. It is sensitive to shadows and sunlight, and signals when these factors change. The iguana can doze in the sunlight, eyes closed, and will react when a shadow passes over the parietal eye.

Salt gland: The green iguana has—as do other iguanas—a salt-excreting gland in its head that drains into the nostrils. This useful gland removes and excretes excess sodium, potassium, and chloride from the blood. The advantage of a salt gland is that it removes these salts while bypassing the kidneys; this means that the salt can be excreted without taking water out of the iguana's system. This helps the iguana avoid dehydration, an issue that will come up later as we learn more about this animal. A salt gland is obviously useful for the marine iguana, which grazes on sea lettuce,

When a salt gland is really useful: The marine iguana of the Galapagos Islands swims through the surf in order to dine on sea algae growing on submerged rocks.

an algae growing on rocks on the ocean floor. The marine iguana can't avoid taking in seawater during this process, and its salt gland maintains the lizard's electrolyte balance in an area where there is little fresh drinking water. The green iguana evolved in an area with seasonal dry spells, and its salt gland helps it deal with seasonal dryness, the decreased moisture in its food, and with the concomitant higher levels of potassium, sodium, and chloride in the diet.

How can you tell if the salt gland is working? Once in a while, you may see salt crystals around a green iguana's nostrils, or a bit of clear exudate from one or both of the nostrils. You may also see dried white crystals on the clear glass of an aquarium. Occasionally, the iguana will sneeze to rid itself of the exudate. The small sneeze and the clear liquid are far different from the lethargic pose and heavy, labored breathing of a respiratory infection, the

reptilian equivalent of pneumonia (see page 114 for more information about respiratory infections).

Senses

Nostrils: The nostrils, of course, are used for normal everyday breathing, but notice the position of the nostrils on a great green iguana.

They are level with the lower edge of the eye, making it possible for the iguana to swim on the surface of the water, eyes above water, and breathe at the same time.

Eyes: Iguanas are visually oriented, meaning that vision takes priority in telling the iguana what's going on, in contrast to a reptile that is audio- or vibration-oriented, like an amphisbaenid (a worm lizard).

Iguanas' eyes contain more cone cells (color-receptive cells that are most effective at high light intensities) than human eyes. This helps explain why iguanas are active during the day (diurnal) and why they prefer to bask high in the tree canopy. Their eyes have fewer rod cells, which perceive shades of gray. If you awaken your iguana at night without turning on the light in the room, you'll find your pet is distinctly uncomfortable at being awakened in low levels of light. The position of the eyes—essentially on opposite sides of the head—means a broad area of vision. Green iguanas will also examine new items by turning their head to use first one eye, and then the other. New food items, in particular, are given a close visual once-over before being cautiously sniffed, then tasted with the tongue.

Jacobson's organ: The sense of smell is served through chemical receptors in the nostrils, as well as by the vomeronasal organ or Jacobson's organ, in the roof of the iguana's mouth. The iguana can detect scent molecules in the air as well as on the ground. As an iguana walks along, it may occasionally lean down and taste the surface on which it is standing. Scent molecules picked up on the surface of the tongue—the saliva is scant and somewhat sticky—are transferred to the Jacobson's organ via the Jacobson's ducts. The molecules are analyzed to determine if the scent comes from a possible predator, food, or another iguana. The scent can determine the sex of another iguana, an important bit of information during the breeding season.

Mouth: The mouth of the iguana is filled with fairly small, even-sized teeth which look like tiny mountains.

These teeth are effective at holding a leaf while the lizard pulls off a piece or simply swallows the leaf whole. Lost or broken teeth are replaced on a regular basis, so at any point, your iguana has between 80 and 120 teeth in its mouth. The number may be impressive, but the teeth, at least those of a young iguana, are too small to offer much of a hazard if you're bitten. This doesn't hold true for the adult iguanas. Adults in breeding season can be aggressive and inflict significant bite-and-yank wounds (see Breeding, Chapter Ten).

Chapter Three

The Great Green Iguana and Its Relatives

Today, because of rather recent realignment of many genera, the family Iguanidae, once one of the largest and most unwieldy assemblages of lizards in the world, is far more cohesive and understandable. The giant green iguana and its relatives constitute this small lizard family.

Meet the Iguanas

There are two kinds of green iguanas. One is the giant green iguana, *Iguana iguana,* found in Central and South America, some West Indian islands, and now the United States.

The other is the Antillean iguana, a large green lizard that looks superficially like a green iguana. It can be easily distinguished from the green iguana (if you have the opportunity to think you might be looking at one) because it lacks the big circular subtympanal scales below the ear opening. The Antillean iguanas *(I. delicatissima)* have no subtympanal scales; green iguanas do.

The Honduran dwarf spiny-tailed iguana, Ctenosaur palearis, *in a defensive pose.*

The Antillean Iguana

The Antillean iguana is found only on the islands of the Antilles. With that limited a range, you can guess what's next—the Antillean iguana is a troubled species, with a decreasing amount of untouched habitat and, traditionally, considered a good food source on its home islands. Although education/conservation programs have been instituted, it's difficult to tell a hunter with a family to feed that Antillean iguanas ought not to be eaten. A few limited breeding programs are in place. The Memphis, San Diego, and Jersey Island (England) zoos are now working with this iguana. Fertile eggs were produced by the lizards, and the first successful hatching occurred in 1997. No Antillean iguanas are known to be in the private sector.

Besides the two species of green iguana in the genus *Iguana*, the new iguana family includes the West Indian (rock) iguanas (*Cyclura*), the neotropical spiny-tailed iguanas (*Ctenosaura*), the desert iguana (*Dipsosaurus*), and the chuckwallas (*Sauromalus*)—from our southwestern

The Antillean green iguana looks much like a green iguana, but lacks the round tympanum, or eardrum, behind each eye.

humans go. Many iguanas have served historically as a food source for native peoples and for visiting sailors/explorers. Today, iguanas are sold, in decreasing numbers, in Latin American markets. The green iguana is said to taste like chicken.

Some iguanas, such as the desert iguanas, are rather extensively insectivorous; some, such as the spiny-tails, are opportunistically omnivorous; others, such as the green iguanas, are essentially herbivorous.

The Relatives

Many, indeed most, of the West Indian rock iguanas of the genus *Cyclura* are considered threatened or endangered. There are about eight species, some with two or more subspecies. All are impressively large lizards with big, expressive eyes, and a dedicated contingent of researchers and breeders.

Rhinoceros iguana: The species of rock iguana seen most frequently in herpetoculture is the rhinoceros iguana, *C. cornuta* ssp. of Hispaniola, a magnificent lizard bearing prominent nubbins on its snout.

Jamaican rock iguana: The most seriously endangered species is the Jamaican rock iguana, *C. collei,* a form thought for several decades to actually be extinct.

Blue rock iguana and Cayman Island rock iguana: One of the most coveted forms is the blue rock iguana, *C. nubila lewisi,* from Grand

deserts and northern Mexico— two genera of Galapagos iguanas (*Amblyrhynchus* and *Conolophus*), and a single genus of Fijian iguanas (*Brachylophus*).

Although many iguanas are terrestrial, some, like the green iguanas, the Fijian iguanas, and some of the spiny-tailed iguanas, are persistently arboreal. In size, these lizards range upward from the foot-long (30 cm) length of the desert iguana, to the more than 6-foot (1.8 m) length of the occasional male green iguana. Despite being the longest species in the family, the green iguana is often surpassed in body bulk by males of some of the stout West Indian iguanas, especially the rhinoceros iguana, *Cyclura cornuta* sp. The chubby-bodied chuckwallas, *Sauromalus* spp., are saxicolous or rock-dwellers. For a lizard, being big has distinct disadvantages, as far as

Cayman Island. The existence of the blue rock iguana is now imperiled by the introduction of and competition from the Cayman Island rock iguana, *C. n. caymanensis*. The latter subspecies, once restricted to Cayman Brac and Little Cayman Island, is now the dominant form on Grand Cayman.

Spiny-tails: The genus *Ctenosaura* (the "C" is silent), the spiny-tailed iguanas, contains both Lilliputian and Brobdingnagian species. There are at least ten species currently recognized, and it seems likely that additional forms will be described. The dwarfed forms, which have proportionately short, clublike tails, can be found in older reference books under their former generic designation of *Enyaliosaurus*. The population numbers of most seem to be holding their own. However, one of the prettiest of the smaller forms,

C. defensor, is reportedly no longer present in some of the areas where it was once rather common.

There are at least three confusingly similar large species established in the United States:

1. A feral population of the Sonoran spiny-tail, *C. hemilopha*, has long been present on the grounds of the Arizona-Sonora Desert Museum in Tucson, Arizona.

2. The black spiny-tail, which, by the way, is saddled with a very inappropriate common name, *C. similis*, seems firmly established in Dade County, Florida, Lee County, Florida, and Cameron County, Texas.

3. The Mexican spiny-tail, *C. pectinata*, has long been actually abundant in Dade County, Florida.

All of these grow to more than 3 feet (91 cm) in length as adults, and although quite terrestrial, can actually climb agilely.

The Fiji banded iguana is endangered, highly protected—and very attractive.

The Allen's Cay Rock iguana, Cyclura cyclura inornata, *can live for 40 years—and needs 12 years to reach sexual maturity.*

Nicaraguan spiny-tail: The only dwarfed form of ctenosaur to appear regularly in the American pet trade is the dwarf Nicaraguan spiny-tail, *C. quinquecarinata*. Adults are about 14 inches (36 cm) long—rarely to 17 inches (43 cm)—and may have a sprinkling of blue scales on their back. This species is often encountered in escarpments and boulder fields from the Isthmus of Tehuantepec (Oaxaca, Mexico) to Nicaragua.

Galapagos iguanas: The iguanas of the Galapagos Islands are of two diverse genera that utilize equally diverse habitats. Because it utilizes the ocean and littoral habitats so prevalent in the Galapagos, one, *Amblyrhynchus cristatus*, is commonly and appropriately known as the marine iguana. It is the only truly marine lizard in the world and feeds exclusively upon marine algae. Some adult males may exceed 5 feet (1.5 m) in total length.

The other Galapagos iguanas are as thoroughly terrestrial as *Amblyrhynchus* is aquatic. These are the two, or perhaps only one, species of land iguanas in the genus *Conolophus*. Of considerable girth, they attain a length of about 3.5 feet (104 cm). They dine largely on the pads of cacti, a food source that is always available on the dry Galapagos islands.

Fijian iguanas: There are three species of Fijian iguanas of the genus *Brachylophus*. These are beautifully colored, smaller lizards, that grow to about 30 inches (76 cm), and are of endangered status.

U.S. desert iguanas: The foot-long (30 cm) desert iguana, *Dipsosaurus dorsalis*, is native to, and easily observed in, the creosote bush belt of western Arizona, southwestern California, southern Nevada, and northwestern Mexico (including Baja). There is but a single species in this genus. It is an alert, terrestrial lizard that is immensely heat-tolerant, remaining surface-active even during the hottest summer weather. It is clad in scales the color of the desert sands, often with highlights of maroon.

Chuckwallas: The chuckwalla is a rock-dwelling lizard that diverges somewhat from the normal outward appearance of iguanas. It has granular scales, a blunt tail tip, and loose skin. When frightened, it sidles into the rock crevices that are omnipresent in its chosen habitats, and inflates its body, a ploy that makes it difficult to remove. The chuckwalla occurs in the creosote bush belt of our southwestern United States and in northwestern Mexico. The lizard is also found on islands near the Baja coast in the Gulf of California. The continued existence of most insular

The Exhuma Island Rock iguana, Cyclura cyclura figginsi, *has been one of the island iguanas the Shedd Aquarium has been studying.*

forms is thought to be tenuous. The exact taxonomic status of these lizards is controversial.

The Mexican spiny-tailed iguana lives in Mexico's savannah woodlands.

Species Table

Common Name	Scientific Name	Origin	Legal Status
Green Iguana	*Iguana iguana*	Latin America	
St. Lucian Green Iguana	*Iguana iguana*	St Lucia Island	
Antillean Green Iguana	*Iguana delicatissima*	Lesser Antilles	
Fijian Banded Iguana	*Brachylophus fasciatus*	Fiji, Tonga Islands	Endangered
Fijian Crested Iguana	*Brachylophus vitiensis*	Fiji	Critically endangered
Fiji Yellow-lipped Iguana	*Brachylopus bulabula*	Fiji	Critically endangered
Galapagos Marine Iguana	*Amblyrhynchus cristatus*	Galapagos Islands	Vulnerable
Barrington Land Iguana	*Conolophus pallidus*	Galapagos Islands	Vulnerable
Galapagos Rosada Iguana	*Conolophus* sp.	Galapagos Islands	Critically endangered
Galapagos Land Iguana	*Conolophus subcristatus*	Galapagos Islands	Vulnerable
Campeche Spiny-tailed Iguana	*Ctenosaura alfredschmiditi*	Campeche, Mexico	Near-threatened
Spiny-tailed Iguana	*Ctenosaura acanthura*	Mexico's Gulf Coast	
Isla de Utila Spiny-tailed Iguana	*Ctenosaura bakeri*	Isla de Utila, Honduras	Critically endangered
Clark's Dwarf Spiny-tailed Iguana	*Ctenosaura clarki*	Michoacan, Mexico	Vulnerable
Yucatan Dwarf Blue-tailed Iguana	*Ctenosaura defensor*	Yucatan	Vulnerable
Yellowback Spiny-tailed Iguana	*Ctenosaura flavidorsalis*	Guatemala to San Salvador	Endangered
Sonora Spiny-tailed Iguana	*Ctenosaura hemilopha*	Pacific Mexico	
Rio Aguan Valley Iguana	*Ctenosaura melanosterna*	Honduras	Critically endangered
Oaxaca Spiny-tailed Iguana	*Ctenosaura oaxacana*	Oaxaca, Mexico	Critically endangered
Isla Roatan Spiny-tailed Iguana	*Ctenosaura oedirhina*	Roatan Island, Honduras	Critically endangered

Base Color	Habitat	Food	Base Size
Green/gray/orange	Forest/savanna	Foliage/flowers	6 feet (1.8 m)
Gray with black cross bars	Forest/savanna	Vegetation	50 inches (127 cm)
Green/gray	Savanna/woodland	Foliage/flowers	6 feet (1.8 m)
Green with blue bands	Savanna/woodland	Foliage/fruit/flowers	2 feet (61 cm)
Green with blue bands	Savanna/beach	Foliage/flowers/fruit	2 feet (61 cm)
Green with white bands	Savanna	Cacti/foliage	35 inches (88 cm)
Black	Seashore	Algae	5 feet (1.5 m)
Tan/olive	Savanna/beach	Cacti/foliage	3 feet (91 cm)
Gray with pink bands	Savanna	Cacti/foliage	4 feet (122 cm)
Tan/olive	Savanna/beach	Cacti/foliage	3 feet (91 cm)
Black/tan	Rocky outcrops	Vegetation/insects	12 inches (30 cm)
Tan/black	Savanna/aridlands	Available vegetation/insects	3 feet (91 cm)
Tan/black	Islandwide	Available vegetation/insects	30 inches (76 cm)
Tan	Savanna/aridlands	Insects/vegetation	1 foot (30cm)
Tan/red/black	Savanna/aridlands	Insects/vegetation	10 inches (25 cm)
Brownish tan	Rocky outcrops	Foliage/insects	12 inches (30 cm)
Tan/black	Savanna/aridlands	Insects/vegetation	30 inches (76 cm)
Brown dorsally/aqua underside	Forest/rocky outcrops	Foliage/insects	31 inches (80 cm)
Brownish tan	Trees	Insects/vegetation	12 inches (30 cm)
Tan/black	Islandwide	Insects/vegetation	30 inches (76 cm)

Species Table (continued)

Common Name	Scientific Name	Origin	Legal Status
Honduran Dwarf Spiny-tailed Iguana	*Ctenosaura palearis*	Honduras, Guatemala	Critically endangered
Mexican Spiny-tailed Iguana	*Ctenosaura pectinata*	Interior and Pacific Mexico	
Dwarf Nicaraguan Spiny-tailed Iguana	*Ctenosaura quinquecarinata*	Southeast Mexico to Panama	Endangered
Black Spiny-tailed Iguana	*Ctenosaura similis*	Southern Mexico	
Booby Cay Rock Iguana	*Cyclura bartschi*	Booby Cay, Bahamas	
Turks and Caicos Rock Iguana	*Cyclura carinata*	Turks and Caicos Islands	Critically endangered
Jamaican Rock Iguana	*Cyclura collei*	Jamaica	Critically endangered
Hispaniolan Rhinoceros Iguana	*Cyclura cornuta*	Hispaniola	Vulnerable
Navassa Island Rhinoceros Iguana	*Cyclura onchiopsis*	Navassa Island; probably extinct (no reported sighting for many years)	Critically endangered
Mona Island Rhinoceros Iguana	*Cyclura stejnegeri*	Mona Island near Puerto Rico	
Andros Island Rock Iguana	*Cyclura cychlura*	Andros Island, Bahamas	Vulnerable
Exuma Island Rock Iguana	*Cyclura cychlura figginsi*	Central and South Exuma Cays, Bahama Islands	
Allen's Cay Rock Iguana	*Cyclura cychlura inornata*	North Exuma Cays	
Sister Isles Rock Iguana	*Cyclura nubila caymanensis*	Little Cayman and Cayman Brac	Critically endangered
Grand Cayman Blue Rock Iguana	*Cyclura nubila lewisi*	Grand Cayman Island	Critically endangered
Cuban Rock Iguana	*Cyclura cychlura nubila*	Cuba and Puerto Rico	Vulnerable
Anegada Island Rock Iguana	*Cyclura pinguis*	Anegada Islands	Critically endangered

Base Color	Habitat	Food	Base Size
Tan	Savanna/woodland	Insects/vegetation	14 inches (36 cm)
Tan/black	Savanna/woodland	Insects/vegetation	4 feet (1.2 m)
Tan/blue	Savanna/woodland	Insects/vegetation	30 inches (76 cm)
Green/tan/black	Savanna/woodland	Insects/vegetation	4 feet (122 cm)
Tan	Islandwide	Insects/vegetation	2 feet (61 cm)
Tan/variable	Most habitats	Insects/vegetation	30 inches (76 cm)
Gray/tan	Hellshire Hills	Insects/vegetation	32–36 inches (81–91 cm)
Tan/black	Low savanna/ woodland	Insects/vegetation	4 feet (1.2 m)
Gray	Forest/rocky outcrops	Vegetation	15 inches (40 cm)
Black/tan	Islandwide	Insects/vegetation	4 feet (1.2 m)
Black/tan	Rocky savanna hillsides and occasionally beaches	Insects/vegetation	34 inches (86 cm)
Tan/black	Islandwide	Insects/vegetation	30 inches (76 cm)
Tan/black	Islandwide	Insects/vegetation	32 inches (81 cm)
Tan/black	Islandwide	Insects/vegetation	40 inches (102 cm)
Tan/black/blue	Islandwide	Insects/vegetation	44 inches (117 cm)
Tan/black	Islandwide	Insects/vegetation	5 feet (1.5 m)
Tan/black	Islandwide	Insects/vegetation	45 inches (114 cm)

Species Table (continued)

Common Name	Scientific Name	Origin	Legal Status
Ricord's Rock Iguana	*Cyclura ricordi*	Hispaniola	Critically endangered
Sandy Cay Rock Iguana	*Cyclura rileyi cristata*	South Exumas	Endangered
Acklins Bight Iguana	*Cyclura rileyi nuchalis*	Acklins Bight, Bahamas	Endangered
San Salvador Rock Iguana	*Cyclura rileyi rileyi*	Cay of San Salvador, Exuma Islands, Bahamas	Endangered
Desert Iguana	*Dipsosaurus dorsalis*	Southwest USA, Northwest Mexico	Least concern
Chuckwalla	*Sauromalus ater*	Southwest USA, Gulf of California islands, Mexico	
Rough-scaled Chuckwalla	*Sauromalus hispidus*	Islands, Gulf of California, Mexico	
San Esteban Chuckwalla	*Sauromalus varius*	Islands, Gulf of California, Mexico	

Base Color	Habitat	Food	Base Size
Tan/black	Islandwide	Insects/vegetation	34 inches (86 cm)
Tan/black	Beach/savanna	Insects/vegetation	2 feet (61 cm)
Tan/black	Rocky areas	Vegetation	23 inches (58 cm)
Tan/black	All suitable habitat	Insects/vegetation	23 inches (58 cm)
Gray/tan	Aridlands/creosote	Flowers/creosote/ other vegetation	13 inches (33 cm)
Tan/black	Rocky areas	Flowers/vegetation	16 inches (41 cm)
Black	Rocky outcrops	Seeds/flowers/vegetation	2 feet (61 cm)
Tan and gray/variable	Rocky outcrops	Seeds/flowers/vegetation	2 feet (61 cm)

Chapter Four

Behavior

Part of the problem with studying green iguanas in the wild is that they look alike. Indulgent owners can identify their pets across the room, but when you're looking at eight iguanas 30 feet (9 m) away through binoculars, they all tend to look pretty much the same.

Identifying Individual Specimens

There are a number of ways to mark or otherwise identify the individual specimens, thanks to researchers who've studied iguana behavior and movement in the field.

1. Crest marks, the placement and form of the spines on the crest, are one way. These spines may be clipped with essentially no discomfort to an iguana to create distinctive individual patterns.

2. Colored beads, sewn along the middorsal crest, are another way to identify individual lizards in the field. Seed beads, about 1/16 inch (2 mm) in diameter, are used for hatchlings. Adults are marked with larger beads, about 1/8 inch (4 mm) diameter, in two

short strings, one on each side of the crest. However, beads are not a long-term solution. As time goes on, at least for desert iguanas, other lizards find the bright beads interesting and they tend to pull at and pull off the colored beads.

3. Reflective paint can be added to the green iguanas' backs in dots, simply to help relocate individual lizards already identity-tagged by other methods. The reflective paint is weakly visible during the day but highly reflective at night. It is very useful for locating iguanas sleeping in the bushes and trees at night, when they can be hand-collected to verify identity if needed. The paint makes the iguanas visible from 90 feet (27 m) or more.

These reflective paint studies have revealed interesting behaviors if the iguanas are disturbed after settling in. Once disturbed at night, adult iguanas vacate that sleeping area. Hatchlings, especially, move considerably higher in the vegetation. The disturbance doesn't have to be anything massive. For the adults, this disturbance can be as simple as nighttime illumination by powerful spotlight, the daytime construction of a blind more than 200 feet (61 m) away, a human

A young adult male giant green iguana emerges after a swim in a Miami canal.

crawling into the trees below the iguanas at night, or the nighttime noosing of two other iguanas. The desire to move away may be partially linked to the iguana's poor night vision; unable to tell exactly what is happening, they hope for safety by moving away from the site.

Movement

Depending on the situation, iguanas can retreat slowly or very quickly. When rapid movement is needed, iguanas can move amazingly fast. They—in fact—most lizards, have a unique ability to sustain short periods of anaerobic activity. This means that iguanas are able to move for a short time without taking in the amount of oxygen needed for that activity; they in effect build up an oxygen debt. Although this sort of activity cannot be sustained for long periods, it can provide what's known as "burst loco-motion"—fast movement over a very short period of time. This enables the lizard to escape danger by darting

away. Iguanas may also escape detection by "freezing" and remaining motionless.

Self-preservation

Iguanas demonstrate most of the 24 identifiable lizard self-preservation behaviors:

1. Selection and preparation of the homesite—Female green iguanas travel considerable distances for communal egg deposition at the same site every year. They dig burrows for egg deposition, and then fill in the burrows to conceal the site.

2. Establishment of territory—Both male and female iguanas establish territories. Large males establish territories and during the breeding season defend not only the territory but all females living within the territory. Their home range also includes at least two seasonally preferred food sources, and sufficient year-round food.

3. Trail making—Not yet described in green iguanas.

4. Marking of territory—Males use secretions from their femoral pores to mark their trails.

5. Showing place preferences— Males in particular select territories that have at least one tree with good perching limbs. Iguanas also select their sleeping site each night.

6. Patrolling territory—By late November, most large males have established their territories. They spend their time resting, displaying, going through courtship bouts—each large male has at least one female sharing his tree—and patrolling. Patrolling consists of short visits to different display posts in the tree, each post change being followed by a signature bob.

7. Ritualistic display in defense of territory, commonly involving the use of coloration and adornments— Male iguanas use posture, erection of their crests, and dewlap expansion to defend their territory and to demonstrate their attractiveness to females. Males become more intensely gold-colored during the breeding season, adding darker tones and accent colors, such as pale blue and orange, to their normal green coloration.

8. Formalized intraspecific fighting in defense of territory—Male iguanas feint-fight with other males to defend their territory. They exchange bobs, become laterally compressed, and push each other, face to face.

9. Triumphal display in successful defense—Not yet described in green iguanas.

10. Assumption of distinctive postures and coloration in signaling surrender—Males will close the lower portion of one eye when a nearby dominant male displays. Males that lose a fight with another iguana darken in color, some within a two-minute period. One deposed male went from a bright orange breeding coloration to brown after being ousted from his displaying post, but when he was able to reclaim his territory, his showy coloration returned.

11. Foraging—Iguanas forage for their diet of leaves and blossoms; they feed in the early morning and in the late afternoon.

12. Hunting—Iguanas are herbivorous and forage, rather than hunt.

13. Homing—Females journey to communal nesting sites, dig burrows and lay their eggs, and then return home. (Some species of dinosaurs also nested communally.)

14. Hoarding—During the breeding season, iguana males monopolize females within their territory by guarding them against intrusions from other, smaller males. Since the females are free to travel from territory to territory, and they do, all the male angst may be for naught.

15. Use of defecation posts— Although no reports indicate green iguanas use defecation posts, iguanas do selectively defecate over water or on a substrate newly swept with water.

16. Formation of social groups— Iguanas form groups that may be described as social, partially

because we can't determine any other reason for them to be together. One example occurs during the dry season. During that season, one of the favored foods is a vine that is abundant. Despite the abundance of this vine, iguanas in a particular study remained in a small portion of the vine-bearing trees. It is possible they preferred to stay in an area where food was obviously abundant, rather than to venture forth and have to find another food source.

17. Establishment of social hierarchy by ritualistic display and other means—Large males select conspicuous perches, and display frequently even outside of the breeding season. These behaviors demonstrate to any female passing through the male's availability.

18. Greeting—There are no reports that deal with iguana greeting rituals, if they exist.

19. Grooming—Iguanas demonstrate little grooming activity. Typical behaviors include scraping the cloaca after defecation and scratching to remove particles clinging to the skin.

20. Courtship, with displays using coloration and adornments—Male iguanas already bear brighter colors during the breeding season. They will display their enlarged jowls and their dewlaps as part of the courtship ritual. Males that are excited, either due to courtship or due to the presence of another male, may become lighter in color.

21. Mating—Males initiate the mating behavior by approaching the possible mate (male or female—the response tells the initiator the sex of the target). The approaching male nods his head and angles his chin to first one side, then the other on the descending part of the bob. If not repulsed by head swings or the retreat of the target, he smells/examines both sides of the target's neck and then seizes one side or the other in his mouth. He moves backward to align his body with the target female and straddles her. If she's receptive, she arches her tail to permit intromission.

22. Breeding and, in isolated instances, attending offspring—Sexually mature male iguanas will repeatedly court females within their territory until they become receptive and copulation is permitted. Multiple copulations are preceded by shorter and shorter courtship bouts. When a male has two receptive females in his territory, he courts each daily but mates each female on alternate days. There are no reports of iguanas tending young, but young iguanas tend to move higher in the canopy, closer to the larger adults, when disturbed at night.

23. Flocking—Hatchling iguanas tend to flock or travel in a group as they begin their hurried dispersal from the nest site. Hatchlings observed in Slothia, a small island in Panama, generally emerge from the nests together, and stay in groups as they approach the southeastern end of the island that serves as the dispersal point.

24. Migration—Female iguanas in Panama migrate to the same egg deposition site each year. How the young hatched at that site return to the site to deposit their own eggs has not yet been determined.

Hatchling Behaviors

Nighttime Emergence

Hatchling and newborn green iguanas are active during the daytime. They sleep in low vegetation, a few feet above the ground.

On the island of Slothia, when the babies emerge from the nesting burrows, they disperse from the nesting site fairly rapidly. Hatching emergence on the island peaks between 11:00 A.M. and noon. Nocturnal emergence was not considered to be significant until a 1978 study by Hugh Drummond and Gordon Burghardt proved otherwise. During the entire 21-day period of observance in May, the nighttime emergence rate was twice that of the daytime rate.

Seeking to discover why the nighttime emergence might be more advantageous than daytime emergence, temperature readings were taken. Temperature probes in the nesting site showed that the nighttime soil temperature at the level of the nest cavity was 82 to 86°F (28–

nas. This predation would be essentially eliminated at night, especially on darker nights when even an individual with dark-adapted vision could not distinguish topographic features of the surroundings.

Daytime Emergence

Hatchlings emerging during the day coordinate their activities. While moving across the clearing toward the dispersal site, they raise their heads repeatedly to scan their surroundings. They also lean down to tongue-flick the substrate. Group movements are led by several individuals or by a single individual hatchling iguana. As they approach the end of the island, some climb reeds to look around, while others explore the shoreline. The movements of the group give, as Gordon Burghardt noted, every indication of vigilance and social interaction. What the iguanas seek with their scanning and tongue flicking, and how they know that the southeast corner of the island is the closest point to the goal of Gatun Island, Panama, isn't yet understood. Visual clues seem to play an important role in deciding what direction to head; when the nest site was surrounded by a low fence, nine out of eleven groups headed in the wrong direction. Orientation may be aided by the brightness of the horizon in the southeasterly direction; the turning of the hatchlings' heads as they scan the nest area is also consistent with the use of magnetic clues by salamanders and pigeons for orientation.

30°C), which matches optimum incubation temperatures for artificial incubation. Hatchlings that emerged at night came out to a cooler temperature of 74 to 78°F (23–26°C). Those that emerge during the day came from a nest site of 82 to 86°F (28–30°C) to an outside temperature of 78 to 86°F (26–30°C) in the shade, and 88 to 99°F (32–37°C) in the full sun. Hatchlings would quickly raise the temperatures of their tiny bodies to 90 to 100°F (33–38°C) the range needed for full digestive and motion function.

What are the advantages of night-time emergence? During the day, visually oriented predation is a major risk. Birds, such as greater anis, and brown basilisk lizards are two of the greater predators on hatchling igua-

Chapter Five

Conservation of Green Iguanas

It has long been realized that many populations of the great green iguana are declining. The reasons behind the declines, until now mostly speculative, are largely human-caused.

Reasons for Declining Populations

Certainly, collection from the wild, both for food and for the pet trade, has played a role in the decline. Even when green iguanas are farmed, wild iguanas are often added to the shipment. Because the shipment is of "farmed" iguanas, no records of numbers are required. In some parts of South and Central America, the eggs are more highly prized than the meat of the green iguana. Gravid females are sold in the *mercados* (the markets) for the eggs they contain, or the iguana hunters noose gravid females and remove their eggs. In both cases, the adult female and her potential young are removed forever from the local iguana population.

Deforestation

Over much of their range, deforestation for homesteads and lumbering interests has had an enormously adverse effect on iguanas.

At one conservation-oriented study site in Panama, forest succession has lessened the overall number of suitable nesting areas.

Green iguanas are "edge-dwellers," living at the buffer edges of forests and streams or forests and cleared areas. In 1960 they were extremely common in the mangrove forests on the Pacific Coast of Mexico; as the forests declined, so did the iguanas. By the end of the 1970s an estimated 5 percent of the population remained, and the vast majority were small adults and adolescents. In El Salvador, destruction of the coastal mangroves and the evergreen forests along streams and collection for the pet market have resulted in the disappearance of the green iguanas from those former habitats. El Salvador's lowland forests have been reduced to one percent of their pre-1950 levels.

Of course, the loss of forest affects all wildlife, not just green iguanas.

The Sister Isles (also called the Cayman Brac) iguana is the more common of the two iguanas found on the Cayman Islands.

The Miami Iguana Population

That green iguanas are adaptable may be easily seen by surveying the population in Miami, Florida. There, in an area of the world far removed from their native neotropical haunts, where the lizards are beset by very unnatural occasional winter freezes, by a large human population crowded into only a few dozen square miles (about 62 km²) of space, and where the lizards have had to learn to subsist on very different dietary plants, hundreds, perhaps thousands, of iguanas exist today. Most residents accept the iguanas as just another, more flamboyant reptilian immigrant. Street signs that say "Speed Kills"

have been erected showing the image of an iguana.

Miami-Dade's population (and that of at least four other counties in Florida) is the result of decades of pet trade discards, escapees, and released pets. The green iguana, plus two species of spiny-tailed iguanas, are now omnipresent in county parks, among greenway and median plantings, even in urban yards and gardens. Since these iguanas hail from many countries, colors and adult sizes are more diverse in Miami than in any area of the lizard's natural range. The breeding males may be clad in scales of orange or green, be barred or plain, have faces flushed with rose or with blue, and be seen breeding with iguanas of very different color and of obviously different provenance.

Conservation Methods

It is now understood that if green iguanas are to remain a viable segment of any country's economy, whether as babies sold for the pet trade or as a coveted food item for native people, adequate methods of conservation must be determined and implemented.

In countries such as Colombia and Peru, both major players in the sale and export of wild-collected iguanas during the fifties, sixties, and seventies, iguanas are now farmed (see pages 48–51) in great numbers. Some babies produced in such situations are head-started (kept in captivity and fed until they are about 12 inches [30 cm] long) and returned to the wild, while others are sold to the pet trade. How

Captive populations of the Jamaican iguana were doubled in 2006 when the Indianapolis Zoo developed a method of incubating the eggs.

effective farming will be in reversing the declines of wild iguana populations remains to be seen. We don't really know how many iguanas an area can support, but new information has helped us to estimate that number with greater accuracy.

Energy demand, as demonstrated by field metabolic rates, helps explain the relationship an animal such as the iguana has with its envi-

Because of feral cats, head start programs for babies of the very rare Anegada iguana raise the young for three years before they are large enough for release.

Lazin' around. An iguana's annual energy requirement is about 2–4 percent of a mammal's.

ronment. It can be used to provide a way to estimate demand on the environment, in terms of food consumption by individual iguanas and the iguana population as a whole. We can then compare the demand of the iguanas with any other species, to see which places less of a "burden" on the environment.

Field Metabolic Rates

It's a little difficult to measure the field metabolic rates (FMR) of free-living creatures. Heart rate telemetry and excretion of radioactive tracers are two methods. Kenneth Nagy, of UCLA, has developed a more reliable method, using doubly labeled water—water in which both the hydrogen and the oxygen have been replaced by isotopes.

Iguana FMR is measured by determining the amount of carbon dioxide given off per gram of body weight. This is measured in the field by capturing the animal, weighing it, and injecting a measured amount of labeled water intraperitoneally. The animals are retained for a few hours, and a blood sample is then taken to measure isotope levels. The animals are released where captured. After a set time period of two to twenty or more days, depending on the predicted isotope loss rate, the animals are recaptured and a second sample of blood or urine is taken for testing. The amount of isotope remaining is used to calculate the lizard's FMR.

The comparisons of annual energy expenditures between a lizard and a mammal are dramatic, when couched in terms of FMRs. When you factor in the number of months per year each animal is active, and correct for differing body mass, the data show the annual energy requirements for a lizard to be 2 to 4 percent of those of the mammal. This is due to three factors:

1. The resting metabolic rate for a lizard is 15 percent of that of a mammal, corrected for differing body mass.

2. Lizards spend about half of each 24-hour period at comparatively low body temperature, which decreases the metabolic rates. For those lizards living in temperate areas, the annual FMR is further reduced because the lizards are inactive during the cold months of the year.

3. For a lizard that is active for more months of the year, such as an iguana, the annual energy requirement as compared to mammals would be higher but still unlikely to leave the single digit percentages.

These differences of FMR between endotherms and ectotherms suggest that a given geographical area could support a greater biomass of endotherms than ectotherms. Because reptiles can obtain more surplus energy from their food than can mammals—there is an enormous energy saving if outside sources of heat, rather than internal heat sources, can be used for body functions—more of that energy can be channeled into growth and reproduction, or to put it bluntly, greater numbers of young, and less time between egg clutch depositions.

Panama Nesting Information

So, if the potential for lots of young is high, what does this mean in terms of conservation? How can we add to the success of hatching? A lot of our information about iguana breeding, nesting, and hatching has come from research groups such as the Organization for Tropical Studies, operators of a research station on Barro Colorado Island in Gatun Lake, Panama, for many years.

The Gatun Lake iguana nesting sites in Panama are probably more intensely studied than any other. The great green iguanas that inhabit the area have, for a number of years, used the same open, sandy nesting sites for egg deposition.

The available areas for nesting—and presumably a number of nesting areas—decreased in 1913 with the construction of the Panama Canal, when lowland forest and riverside land was flooded. Since then, the canal locks have stabilized water levels in the lake and prevented the formation of the sandy water-eroded banks and beaches in and on which iguanas would normally nest. Since the forest was protected at the same time, the abandoned cleared fields in the surrounding forest have largely succeeded, further reducing suitable iguana nesting sites.

In mid-dry season, Gatun-area female iguanas congregate both at existing natural sites as well as at a few widely separated artificial clearings to lay their eggs. Nesting sites on small islands seem to be more successful, probably because they lack resident predators. The same females return year after year to these sites. It has been found that gravid Gatun Lake female iguanas travel up to 4,650 feet (1,400 m) to return to their nesting sites. However, the average travel distance is 1,375 feet (425 m).

Hatchlings disperse from the nesting sites to areas they deem habitable, and stay close to those areas. They stay near the water, in typical iguana edge-dweller fashion. Like sea turtles, the female hatchlings will return to the site of their own hatching when the time comes for them to lay their own eggs.

In Gatun Lake, three nesting sites are on islands adjacent to Barro Colorado Island: Slothia, a tiny island off the northwestern coast of the island, Mosca, a small island off the southeastern coast, and DeLessups, off the northern tip of the island. Slothia is especially convenient because the nesting clearing is visible from one of the porches of the research station.

On each of these islands, the same females, and their matured daughters, return year after year to lay their eggs. Electrophoresis has shown that populational differences exist between the iguanas using these sites, indicating that the lizards and their sites were discrete long before the creation of the lake. Although the accumulated data can tell us that these iguana populations are, in effect, isolated from each other, it cannot identify what has made a particular site attractive.

Even within relatively small regions, different populations of great green iguanas are known to differ in growth rates, nesting behavior, and in timing of the breeding cycle. The electrophoretic results on the Gatun Lake iguanas indicate that populational differences are genetic as well. Although researchers concerned with repopulating traditional iguana habitats would prefer to, and should, maintain area-specific gene pools, this may not be needed for success. The multipopulational and multigenerational iguanas in Miami indicate that, if absolutely necessary, breeding and reintroduction programs can succeed, even if diverse breeding stock was used.

Efficiency in Egg Hatching

Preferably, the replenishing of iguanas in areas where they previously existed will utilize large numbers of populationally matched hatchlings to release into the wild. All that takes is a high hatch rate from eggs from that site. The hatching of iguana eggs in captivity is now a rather routine procedure; however, some insight as to why certain techniques work has

Female iguanas in the wild thermoregulate by basking.

been gained as the result of research by John Phillips, Anthony Garel, and other herpetologists.

Moisture and Temperature Variations

Their experiments on green iguana eggs indicate that both moisture and temperature variations during incubation alter the length of incubation and the size of the young. Eggs from several females in one population in Belize were incubated on vermiculite substrate with varying amounts of water. One half were incubated at 84°F (29°C), the other half at 87°F (31°C). Eggs were half-buried in the dampened vermiculite to permit water exchange in both vapor and liquid form. Eggs and their containers were weighed every 14 days and any lost water replaced in the substrate.

The eggs kept at 84°F (29°C) began to hatch after 94 days, and those kept warmer, at 87°F (31°C), began to hatch after 90 days. Hatching ratios at the two temperatures were identical. Eggs kept on the wet substrate may have been slightly more successful in hatching than eggs on drier media, but the hatching rate in both cases was no lower than 90 percent, already better than the 50 percent expected in the wild.

Following deposition, viable eggs kept on relatively dry substrate generally increased gradually in weight for 60 days, and then got lighter as hatching time approached. Those kept on wetter substrate got increasingly heavier for 84 days,

Captive breeding techniques have enabled us to captive-raise green iguanas, for reintroduction and for the pet market.

then began to lose weight. The latter "wetter substrate" eggs took up to seven days longer to hatch than eggs kept on dry to moist media.

This experiment shows that successful incubation of iguana eggs depends to a large extent on the environment that surrounds the eggs once they are laid. The optimum incubation temperature for the green iguana is about 86°F (84–87°F). Embryos exposed to extreme cooler or warmer temperatures, or too little or too much moisture, often die. Those embryos incubated near the low end of the temperature range take longer to reach full term than those incubated at warmer temperatures, generally use more of the egg yolk before they hatch, and are larger in SVL (snout-vent length) as a result. Besides hatching in fewer days, embryos incubated at warmer, drier temperatures are smaller and must rest and absorb the unused yolk before they move out of the nesting area. It is to the embryos' advantage to be larger and not to be burdened with extra yolk to absorb after hatching in order to avoid nest predators and evade pursuers.

Iguana Farming

Only 30 years ago, the captive breeding of lizards was a comparatively new discipline. At that time, the vast majority of the specimens of all lizard species entering the pet trade were collected from the wild. Over the next few years, hobbyists learned a great deal about breeding all reptiles, particularly snakes, and with each passing year, a greater percentage of the pet trade reptiles came from these diligent and talented herpetoculturists. Our knowledge regarding the herpetocultural needs of lizards has improved, but we still know more about breeding snakes than lizards.

The Pro Iguana Verde Foundation

The Pro Iguana Verde Foundation in Costa Rica manages buffer zones to increase the habitat and the fauna populations. Farmers raise, release, and hunt iguanas, and produce iguana leather products and handicrafts. During the first five years of operation, 80,000 green iguanas were raised and released into the forest.

It became evident 40 or more years ago that hatchling green iguanas had the potential of becoming popular "pets." Even then, tens of thousands were imported each year from Colombia, Guyana, and Peru. All were collected from the wild.

When, in the early 1960s, I (RDB) began journeying periodically to Latin America to purchase wholesale quantities of tropical fish and reptiles for the pet distribution company for which I was then working, one of the first things I saw was a compound filled with rows of 8-foot cubed (2.4 m) wire cages, and in each cage were hundreds to thousands of baby iguanas. The babies sold then for only a few cents apiece, and again, each and every one had been taken from the wild.

Since those early years, we have watched the availability of baby iguanas in the pet trade wax and wane. In some years, seemingly uncountable thousands would be available. In the next, far fewer would appear in the pet trade.

It seemed that the supply of these charming lizards from the wild was no longer as dependable as in the early days, and population fluctuations affected more than just the pet industries of the world. Green iguanas were, and are, important food animals in virtually all Latin American countries, where both the lizards and their eggs are eaten. The exporting countries began to scrutinize reptile populations and to formulate exportation laws. Colombia decided to disallow the exportation of the lizards, they became difficult to get from Peru, and Mexico closed the doors on wildlife exports. In fact, the availability of baby green iguanas in the 1980s was rather like the bouncing of a rubber ball—readily available, rarely available, abundant, unavailable—up and down, up and down. During these years, as pet dealers clamored for more baby iguanas, iguana farming began. Agreements were hammered out: So many captive-hatched babies would be returned to the wild; the rest would be sold to the pet dealers.

Beginning Stages of Farming

At first, the term farming was rather laughable. It simply meant that gravid female wild iguanas were captured, held captive until they laid their eggs, the eggs were allowed to incubate, then the babies—sometimes after undergoing a headstart program (see page 43), sometimes not—were released or sold. It accomplished little more than allowing a farm to comply with the letter, but not the conservation-oriented intent, of the new laws. This went on for many years, but all the while, the iguana farmers were learning that if wild populations were rebounding at all, they were doing so slowly, and that if certain concepts were employed, iguanas really *could* be farmed in the truest sense of the word.

Changes in Farming

Now, wild adult iguanas of both sexes were collected, caging was

A captive-bred young iguana is exposed to human contact as soon as the lizard leaves the egg. Such a lizard is more adaptable to captivity than a wild animal stressed by capture and handling.

improved, diet was carefully delved into, and *voilà*—after some initial setbacks, green iguanas were really being farmed. Many farms were in Colombia, some were in Venezuela, and some in El Salvador; others were elsewhere. By the early 1990s, baby green iguanas were again available to the pet trade, but this time with a vengeance as 600,000 to more than a million a year were sold to American pet dealers!

Iguana farming has been eminently successful in Latin American countries. The iguanas were preadapted to climate, to photoperiod, to virtually everything but caging, diet, and population concentrations. Fortunately, the lizards have proven adaptable; more despite what we've done, rather than because of what we've done, the captive iguanas have thrived and bred.

Few American iguana owners will bother with breeding their giant green iguanas and raising the young for the pet market—most pet stores simply want the cheapest iguana possible.

Formulas for Success

Each iguana farm has its own formula for success. Some still augment their captive-breeding programs by seeking and accepting gravid female iguanas from the wild. Some farms claim now to be entirely self-contained, needing no new wild-collected breeders. Some use huge net cages; others simply ring in vast areas of suitable habitat with heavy metal walls that form open-top cages. Some of these latter cages may be several hundred feet (more than 30 m) in length and almost as wide. Since green iguanas are rather proficient burrowers, the caging materials often extend a yard (91 cm) below the surface of the ground.

Some farms segregate their iguanas by size, and except during the breeding season, by sex. Others may keep the sexes together, but segregate the young from the older iguanas to prevent predation.

Most of the farms leave the eggs in the ground to undergo natural incubation, and run down, catch, and remove the babies as they hatch. If hatchings are really good, up to several thousand baby iguanas may be hatched each season. Some farms hold the babies for a few days to a few weeks before shipping them, but other farms may sell the hatchlings almost as soon as they absorb their yolk and leave the eggs.

Farming in the United States

Because labor and facilities are comparatively cheap in most Latin American countries, the vast quantities of hatchling great green iguanas produced were so inexpensive American herpetoculturists could not compete. Thus, the comparatively few great green iguanas that are produced in this country are bred, one clutch at a time, by hobbyists who have found themselves with a pair of the lizards and who wish to experi-

The International Iguana Society

IIS is a broad-vista organization dedicated to the preservation of the biological diversity of iguanas through habitat preservation, conservation, research, captive breeding, and communication (see Useful Addresses and Literature, page 147).

ence firsthand the satisfaction that accompanies the successful culmination of a breeding program. In other words, in the United States, the breeding of green iguanas for the foreseeable future is simply an aspect of successful herpetoculture rather than a money-making venture.

Iguana Rescue Services

Until a very few years ago, iguana rescue organizations were virtual unknowns. The sad truth was that until the late 1980s and the 1990s, we as hobbyists knew so very little about the actual needs of iguanas that few of the lizards lived long enough to need the services of a caring rescuer. Today, however, things are very different. When fed the correct diet and given sufficient space, iguanas not only grow incredibly fast, but are routinely living longer than a dog or cat! Many great green iguanas easily attain a longevity of 15 years, and there is no reason to believe that a life span of 20 or more years will not be reached by iguanas that are particularly well cared for. Naive owners realized they possessed a creature that needed more than they were willing or able to supply. Suddenly, many of these wonderful lizards were discarded when their natural behaviors became annoying.

Even the most well-meaning purchasers may ultimately find that for one reason or another they can no longer care for their iguana. The first step most of these people take is to place an ad in the classified section of their local newspaper. Perhaps the lizard will be adopted by another caring person, perhaps not, and it is the "perhaps not" that has created the very much-needed iguana rescue services.

In an effort to learn a little more about the machinations of an iguana rescue service, we asked one individual in Florida about the rescue organization she and a friend started several years ago.

One of the first things our contact revealed was that because of financial constraints, they could no longer accept any unwanted iguanas, but they would be more than happy to provide iguana information and to try to help an owner place the lizard he or she could no longer keep.

Questions About Rescue Services

1. How do owners find this rescue service? It is, we were told, just one of many, with an Internet address. When we looked, sure enough, there it was, sandwiched among rescue services in Arizona, Colorado, Connecticut, New York, and other states.

2. How many iguanas can a rescue service handle at one time? Far too few, but they all do the best they can with very limited, usually personal, out-of-pocket financing.

3. Who gives up an iguana? There were many avenues—from adults who had inherited the lizard from a college- or service-bound offspring,

Many iguana rescue services find their available space quickly taken up by discarded iguanas, and their resources by iguanas with chronic health issues.

demeanor of an adult male iguana captivated the imagination of many folks who were quick to offer the big lizard a home, even after having been told of the problems possible from such an adoption. To avoid placing an iguana, only to have it given back after a few months; potential "adopters" are screened carefully and there is an adoption fee.

6. Are more iguanas in need of help at certain seasons? Indeed they are. The onset of winter brought many iguanas to the rescuers from owners not wanting to face the problem of keeping the lizards warm.

7. Does the rescuer, we asked, feel that most pet stores are remiss in informing potential customers of the true needs of a green iguana? The answer was an unequivocal yes.

8. Had the rescue services been offered species other than green iguanas? We were surprised to hear no, no desert or spiny-tailed iguanas had ever been rescued, but these creatures have a monetary value in the reptile pet market.

9. Our final question was, what was the health problem most often found in the rescued iguanas. Again, the answer was unequivocal—diet.

from parents who had tired of caring for their small child's pet, from graduating college students moving on into the real world, and from kids themselves who no longer wanted the responsibility of caring for an often less-than-fully tame, growing lizard.

4. Does their rescue service meet the demands for their services in their community? Absolutely not, not even with many folks offering foster homes.

5. Is it harder to place adults than babies? We were surprised to be told no. Our contact said that the size and impressive, at times haughty,

Conservation of Other Iguanas

Despite having reduced numbers, populations of the great green iguana are in good shape compared to populations of other iguanas, especially those that are endemic to only one or two small islands. Many of these vulnerable species are threatened or endangered. The actual population statistics of other mainland iguanas remain undetermined.

• The Antillean green iguana, *Iguana delicatissima*, seems to be diminishing in numbers on its small homeland islands. It is conjectured that competition with the introduced great green iguana, crossbreeding with the green iguana, and habitat degradation are the causes behind the reduced numbers. Captive breeding attempts with this species have limited success.

• All three species of the Fijian iguanas of the genus *Brachylophus* (see page 24) are endangered, but two are being successfully bred in small numbers in captivity.

• Both species of the Galapagos land iguanas (genus *Conolophus*) are considered endangered. Captive breeding and habitat protection programs seem to be helping to stabilize the populations.

• The Utila Island spiny-tailed iguana, formerly called the Isla de la Bahia spiny-tail, *Ctenosaura bakeri*, is now thought to occur only on Utila Island. Captive-breeding programs on Utila Island, sponsored by the Zoological Society of Frankfurt and the Senckenberg Museum, are underway to stabilize the population. However, programs of mangrove cutting and swampland draining on the island have caused the conservation organizations a great deal of concern. The International Iguana Foundation

has formed Project *Ctenosaura* to implement conservation measures for threatened *Ctenosaura* species.

• The Yucatan dwarf spiny-tailed iguana, *Ctenosaura defensor*, now seems extirpated or rare where it was once common; however, actual population statistics are currently lacking.

An adult male iguana may remain tractable to handling—or may not. Taking the iguana into sunlight increases the likelihood of being scratched.

Mexican spiny-tailed iguana, Ctenosaura pectinata, *is a member of the largest genus of iguanas. At least five of the 17 species are critically endangered.*

• Several species of rock iguana of the genus *Cyclura* remain threatened and, because of their limited ranges, are certainly vulnerable to climatic or other catastrophes. Among these are the Booby Cay rock iguana, *C. carinata bartschi*, the Turks and Caicos rock iguana, *C. c. carinata*, the Mona Island rhinoceros iguana, *C. cornuta stejnegeri*, the Andros Island rock iguana, *C. cychlura cychlura*, the Exuma Island rock iguana, *C. c. figginsi*, the Allen's Cay rock iguana, *C. c. inornata*, the Sister Isles rock iguana, *C. nubila caymanensis*, the Cuban populations of the Cuban rock iguana, *C. n. nubila*, the Sandy Cay rock iguana, *C. rileyi cristata*, and the Acklins Bight Island rock iguana, *C. r. nuchalis*. Many of these are now being bred in captivity by private hobbyists and zoos. Although it is doubtful that captive breeding will favorably impact wild populations, these programs can serve as a Noah's Ark, at least temporarily.

• Populations of several of the rock iguanas are seriously enough reduced to have the lizards listed as endangered. These species are the Jamaican rock iguana, *C. collei*, the Grand Cayman blue rock iguana, *C. nubila lewisi*, the Anegada Island rock iguana, *C. pinguis*, and the San Salvador rock iguana, *C. rileyi rileyi*. Habitat degradation, competition with feral dogs, cats, and other animals, and intergradation with other introduced subspecies have led to the decline of these lizards.

• A recovery program now in place for the Jamaican rock iguana enlisted the aid of a major shoe manufacturer. In answer to an appeal from the recovery team at the Sedgwick County Zoo (Wichita, Kansas), Nike designed and constructed 15 abrasion-resistant vests to hold the radio transmitters needed to track the lizards; after all, who knows better about abrasion than a sports shoe manufacturer? If the tiny garments prove successful, Nike has offered 50 more. The Jamaican rock iguana was long thought to be extinct, but a population believed to number fewer than 200 individuals was discovered in 1990. Captive-breeding programs are now extant on Jamaica and at a few zoos in the United States.

Chapter Six

Choosing and Taming a Green Iguana

Iguanas are one of the few lizards that are more readily available from your local pet store than from specialty breeders. It is the very low prices asked for these imported lizards that keeps their availability thus skewed. The advantage to buying a green iguana from a specialty breeder is that specialty breeders keep track of their animals' lineage, and breed for color, size—either small or large—and behavioral characteristics such as gentleness and calmness. Imported lizards are simply that—imported in large numbers and not bred for any particular characteristic.

What to Choose

Domestically Bred Hatchlings

Our suggestion is to buy domestically bred iguana hatchlings when they are available; these have probably endured less stress for a shorter time than others. They are often a little more expensive than other iguanas, but they are well worth the price difference. Economically speaking, the domestic breeder of the hatchling is rewarded for breeding his or her animals, incubating the eggs, raising up the hatchlings (see Breeding, page 122), and finding a buyer. The buyer nets the rewards in acquiring an animal that is used to captivity, used to human attention, and feeds well on easily obtained foods.

Farm-produced Iguanas

If domestically hatched iguanas are not available, buy one that is farm-produced. Your pet store usually will know if the iguanas it is offering are farm-produced. Farm-produced iguanas are good business for iguana food manufacturers. Farm producing not only ensures a consistent grade of animal, but also helps assure the iguana food manufacturers of a steady supply of iguanas that will help create a greater demand for their food. But there's the conservation angle as well: Iguanas have become such a popular pet and food item (for meat and for eggs) in Panama and in Costa Rica that the native populations themselves have

become severely reduced. Grass-roots programs have been started that provide young iguanas to families to raise, much like providing families with a few chickens to raise for eggs and for food.

Wild-collected Iguanas

Wild-collected iguanas should be purchased only if neither domestically nor farm-bred iguanas are available. A baby taken from the wild, if it survives to reproductive age, means one less adult to replenish native stocks. On an individual basis, wild-collected babies have been stressed more severely and for longer than captive-bred or farm-raised babies. The immune systems of the wild-caught hatchlings are more apt to be already compromised than those of iguanas from the other two categories.

With time, your iguana will associate your presence with good things—like food.

The chocolate brown bars on the side of a baby iguana help break up its silhouette to potential predators in the wild.

Signs of a Healthy Iguana

• A healthy iguana is alert, has good color, and has good body weight.

• Healthy baby iguanas are green—vibrant and intense, like healthy leaves of a growing plant—blue-green or, rarely, a grayish green. A dull pasty green, deep olive-green, or yellow-green usually indicates poor health or impending death.

• Some baby iguanas have contrasting coloration. They may bear prominent, darker, vertical bars of brown, rust, or gold. The barring is usually strongest anteriorly. The markings near the neck and shoulder are usually the most evident; they tend to fade, but not disappear, with age.

A healthy iguana responds to positive stimuli such as a bright UVA/UVB light and warmth.

• A healthy baby iguana should have bright eyes, and watch the movements around it, even as you hold it. And if among those alert, bright-eyed babies, there is one that is calm, or at least relatively so, when you reach in its cage, choose it. The more nervous a baby iguana is, the harder it will be to tame it!

Darkened nuchal scales (the raised scales on the neck) may indicate stress.

• When lifted and alerted, a healthy iguana will, except for an occasional quizzical head tilt, try to keep its head almost level with the horizon. An ill iguana is less apt to do so.

• Never, not even for humanitarian reasons, choose an iguana with dull, sunken eyes and listless mien. It will probably not survive.

• Always choose an iguana from a clean cage that has been provided with ample fresh drinking water and a warmed and well-illuminated basking area.

• If there are dead iguanas in the cage, walk out. This pet store is not for you.

Colors

Great green iguanas are brightest at hatchling size. The brilliance may be retained until the iguana is nearly one-third grown, but it does, eventually, naturally fade. It is thought that because the baby iguanas inhabit the lower levels of the forest, the brilliant green of both dorsal and ventral surfaces helps camouflage and protect the lizards from predators. As the lizards grow, they naturally become more efficient at evading predators and less dependent on camouflage for survival. In fact, the colors assumed by some iguanas make the lizards stand out boldly from their backgrounds of leaves and branches.

The overall ground color of a baby great green iguana is something of a stress barometer. A healthy, basically nonstressed baby is a vibrant green. Variable by population, there may be a nuchal (neck) and a shoulder saddle of dark brown, light charcoal, or gold (the latter with darker edges anteriorly). There may or may not be additional dark lateral blotching, but there is almost invariably dark caudal (tail) banding. There may be indication of turquoise ventrolateral (the sides of the belly) barring. Some babies are quite blue in color.

A cold baby iguana is often an unpleasant dark green to olive green. It should be brought to optimum body temperature—94 to 100°F (34–37.8°C)—as quickly as possible.

This can be done by bathing it in body-deep warm water. A cold iguana will be motion and response impaired. Do not let it drown.

A too-warm baby iguana will be a lighter than normal green, often with an even paler head color. Overheating will kill an iguana as surely as overchilling will. Watch cage and transportation bag temperatures carefully.

A sick baby iguana may initially be an unpleasant and unnatural dark green, but as death nears, may turn a sickly yellowish color.

The ground color of adult iguanas, especially males in breeding raiment, is more varied than that of the babies or that of adult females. The ground color of many healthy adult iguanas is bluish to greenish gray. They may retain evidence of the dark shoulder saddle, dark ventrolateral

An albino adult green iguana.

Surprisingly enough, red iguanas have green bellies.

bars, and the tail is usually noticeably dark banded, at least for the distal two thirds of its length.

Unhealthy adults may take on a yellowish tinge. Cold adults are darkest, sometimes very dark. Overheated adults are very light, often with an almost white head.

During the breeding season, sexually mature males may turn, partially or entirely, a dark forest green, a light orange, or a brilliant fire orange. The ground color of others may change little, but the jowls and/or the anterior vertebral crest may become suffused with rose or orange. Following the breeding season, the brilliant colors are often muted.

Color morphs: New color morfs, such as hypomelanism (reduced black resulting in a pale green overall coloration), are being developed.

Albinos were the first color morphs developed in captive-bred green iguanas, but the great numbers of green iguanas being ranched in El Salvador and other countries pretty much meant that any unusual color morphs would be spotted and placed into a development program. Fluker Farms for instance, offers hatchling yellow and brick red morphs. In 2009, the red babies retailed for $70–$150, the yellows for $90–$200, and the albinos for $200–$500.

Although albino, red, and leucistic iguanas seem to react in normal iguana manner to most stimuli, it would seem prudent to offer albinos more sheltered areas (for protection from direct sunlight) than a normally colored iguana might need. The lack of normal pigmentation in the eye and skin may cause a great deal of discomfort, especially in brilliantly lit situations.

Color Changes with Age

As green iguanas grow, they lose the intensity of color that typifies the healthy young. They tend to dull down in color once they reach the 3-foot (91 cm) length. Nonbreeding adults are often predominantly grayish green, but may be pale orange or, more rarely, bright orange. Many retain at least some of the dark markings they had as juveniles.

Handling the Baby Iguana

You want a baby iguana that has been handled and had some attention paid to it. When we bought a baby iguana in our local pet store, it was obvious that someone had really worked with the entire cageful. These iguanas were alert and wolfing down their meal of chopped and mixed romaine/green beans/shredded carrots; their cage had a bright basking light suspended over the feeding area, and the iguanas didn't panic when the cage was opened and we reached in to lift out one of the babies.

Handle the baby you're interested in buying, and look at it closely. Do not purchase one that has the bones—especially the pelvic girdle—

Touched gently under the throat, a baby iguana opens his mouth. He has no idea what to expect from humans. Handle with care.

starkly evident. Look at the overall color, and especially around the eyes; sunken, dark eyes are a very bad sign. Do not buy one that has

A tame male iguana accepts a gentle touch on the head, but he isn't certain he likes it. Only do this with an iguana you know is used to humans.

dried or smeared feces around the vent; this is a symptom of an intestinal problem such as coccidia, and a confirmation that this iguana already has lowered resistance. Healthy iguanas wipe their vents on the substrates after they defecate. An iguana that doesn't perform this instinctive action may have serious problems.

The "torpedo hold" presses the iguana's legs against the body so he cannot use his feet to scratch—but should he choose to wriggle, continuing to hold him will be very difficult.

Determining the Sex of Iguanas

Sexing the Juvenile Iguana

Semi-adult iguanas can be sexed by secondary characteristics, but these aren't apparent in hatchling iguanas.

Note: A company named Zoogen, in Davis, California, developed an iguana-sexing technique using DNA from a drop of blood, but there hasn't been enough demand to continue the service.

If you really need to know the sex of your juvenile iguana, there are two methods, developed by researchers Jesus Rivas and Tito Avila, which seem to work equally well:

1. Probing the juvenile to determine the depth of the cloacal pouch. The juvenile iguana is held upside down and one hind leg is held adjacent to the tail. A lubricated probe is gently inserted into the cloaca, and the depth it will go is recorded in millimeters or the equivalent to a given number of femoral pores. For hatchling females with a body length (snout-vent length) from 3 to $3\frac{1}{2}$ inches (68–78 mm), the cloacal pouch measures $\frac{1}{16}$ to $\frac{2}{16}$ of an inch deep (1–2 mm), with the mean being $\frac{3}{32}$ of an inch (1.51 mm). Males of the same snout-vent length have cloacal pouches measuring $\frac{2}{16}$ to $\frac{5}{16}$ of an

Do not select this iguana. This iguana is very thin and displays a color typical of an iguana that is desperately ill and too cold.

inch (2–3.5 mm), and the mean is ⁴⁄₁₆ of an inch (2.61 mm).

2. For iguanas one year old or less, there is hemipenial eversion. As with snakes, this only works on *very young* iguanas. Iguanas older than a year are better sexed by the depth of the cloacal pouch, because it is very difficult to evert their hemipenes without damaging them permanently. Hemipenial eversion is accomplished by holding the animal upside down and applying soft pressure on both sides of the base of the tail, pressing toward the head. Opening the cloaca slightly may help. If hemipenes evert, the lizard is a male.

Sexing the Older Iguana

Male and female iguanas can be so similar in external appearance that even experienced iguana keepers have been fooled (Rex's owner, a long-time iguana keeper, knew Rex was male, until "he" began laying eggs). The differences are easier to discern if you have several iguanas to compare. Males generally are bulkier. Males generally have higher crests than females, and their dewlap is larger. Males have larger femoral pores on the underside of the hind legs than do females. During breeding season, males flush with brighter colors than the females, their temporal areas swell, and they develop a chip on their shoulder.

Which Sex Makes the Better Pet?

A tame iguana is a tame iguana, and there seem to be no differences between the tameness of males and the tameness of females during non-breeding season. Either can make a good pet, if you are willing to let the iguana's natural behavior become your standard for good behavior. If you want to breed your iguana, you'll need a pair, or you'll want "borrowing" privileges for the sex you don't have. Both sexes can be problematic during the breeding season; females can ovulate and become egg-bound (even with no male around!) and males can be aggressive toward their owners.

Young or Adult?

Pick a young iguana. Sadly, unless they have been hand-raised and are tame, most sub-adult and adult iguanas are not good candidates for pets. Most are far more difficult to acclimate to captivity than the hatchlings, fleeing and banging into the sides of their cages at the approach of a human. Adults hardly get along with each other in enclosed areas, much less with humans. If you place more than one adult in a cage, particularly if two or more are males, the hierarchy between/among them means that the choicest basking area and first-feeding rights go to the most dominant. Subordinates may not feed, even when there is plenty of food present.

Wild adults are also extremely resistant to being handled. They know how to use their claws and tail in defense, and seem to forget more easily that being handled by a human does not mean death.

Taking Your Iguana Home

Once you have selected your young iguana, don't be concerned if its colors seems to change once you've handled it. It is natural for a newly grasped, frightened iguana to fade somewhat in color, or that parts of the head and crest should darken with stress. The pointed scales on the neck and the head, and crest scales of our young male iguana turned almost black when we handled him; we hadn't known until then that the crest scales contained chromatophores and so were capable of color changes. Once left to its own devices, the iguana's brilliant green coloration should soon return.

Carry your iguana home quickly in a cloth bag, keeping it at a suitable temperature while in transit. During hot weather never leave the lizard (or any animal!) in a closed car or sitting in the sun. If the iguana is transported during the winter, keep it next to your body, in a warm vehicle, or moderate winter's temperatures by using a chemical hand warmer in the box or bag along with your iguana.

Once you're home, take the iguana out of its bag or box and place it in its cage. Make certain there's fresh drinking water in the cage, turn on the overhead light, and leave the iguana alone for a few hours, or even until the next day. You can put food in the cage, but the chances are your iguana will be far too upset to eat.

Add food to the cage later that day, or wait until the next day. Iguanas are active in the mid-morning, and again in the early afternoon, and do most of their feeding during these times.

Taming Your Iguana

You can begin taming your iguana once it has begun eating, but do not expect an immediate positive response. Do not expect the responses of an iguana to you or its surroundings to be like those of a domestic mammal or an easily tamable bird. Some iguanas resist all overtures by their human keepers, never becoming tame. With much dedicated work by their owner, some iguanas may become reasonably tame, yet resist handling, while others become completely docile and allow their keepers nearly any degree of liberty they choose to take.

It can take a concerted effort on your part to truly tame an iguana, and even then, some iguanas have "bad days," days when they simply do not want to be bothered. In the wild, the survival instinct dictates that the touched or grasped iguana must either flee or fight. In captivity, this very strongly programmed instinct must be overcome.

Iguanas don't really want to live closely together, even with other iguanas. By nature, iguanas are rather solitary creatures. Their paths may cross, they may share trees, they get together during the breeding season, and then only to breed. This is especially true of males. It is the most dominant ones that have the greatest success in breeding. To assert dominance they display, lash with their tail, and in a real "knock down, drag out fight," they may bite and use their claws as well. Females

are less territorial but may indulge in hierarchical behavior.

Most iguanas will strenuously fight an immobilizing method of restraint. To survive in the wild, an iguana must be alert, and know when to choose flight over threat—flight does save energy. Despite their large size, even adult iguanas are usually very quick to dash to the comparative safety of the trees or the water if approached. They may catapult themselves from high perches if startled, landing with a considerable thud on the ground and scuttling away, or simply drop from an overhanging limb into the water and rapidly swim from the source of the disturbance.

Gaining Your Lizard's Confidence

Learning from these behaviors, there are some methods that may help you gain the confidence of your lizard:

• Until your iguana is completely used to its new home and to you, always move very slowly. You will soon learn what your iguana will tolerate and what it is more reluctant to allow. Then you can concentrate on overcoming the negative responses.

• Remember that many iguanas will resist being grasped from above. If you wish to lift your iguana, approach it slowly and induce it to step onto your hand or arm. Once it is clinging securely, restrain the iguana with your other hand, if necessary, to prevent it from falling or jumping. You will be able to move more quickly as your iguana becomes accustomed to this procedure. For a while, you may need to hold its hind legs next to its body with one hand and the front legs against its body with the other hand. This not only keeps the iguana within your reach, but protects your hands and arms from being scratched by its claws.

• If your iguana refuses to allow you to touch it or to be held in your hand, try the same exercise with a thin stick wrapped with cloth at the tip. Some iguanas initially find this a more acceptable alternative than hand touching. If your iguana will allow this, shorten the stick a little every three or four days until you can at last discard it and your hand is touching your iguana.

Slow, repetitive movements on your part should soon lead to more satisfactory iguana-owner interactions. Always remember, however, that even tame iguanas can be rather easily startled and may drop from your arm or shoulder. Landing on an artificial surface such as a carpeted floor can break bones. An unrestrained iguana should never be taken outside; when startled or stimulated by the sunlight into hyperawareness, it can leap off and disappear under a house, up a tree, or into a yard before you've realized what has happened. If your iguana is semitame, one of the iguana leashes carried in most pet stores will help you keep it under control.

Husbandry of Other Pet Iguanas

Besides the great green iguana, there are chuckwallas, desert iguanas, spiny-tailed iguanas, and several species of rock iguana readily available in the American pet trade. Chuckwallas and desert iguanas are from the U.S., the spiny-tails are of Latin American origin, and the rock iguana, more properly called the rhinoceros iguana, is from Hispaniola.

Ctenosaurs

Although often thought of as terrestrial or saxicolous (land or rock-dwelling) species, most of the spiny-tails are also agile climbers that ascend to considerable heights in trees, and some, such as the dwarfed forms, tend to seek refuge high above the ground in hollowed limbs or cactus skeletons when startled. Once alerted, spiny-tails are difficult to approach, often sidling quietly around a tree trunk or darting into a rock crevice in an effort to avoid being seen. They may also splay and flatten themselves against a tree trunk or atop large horizontal limbs where they then look more like an irregularity in the tree than a live lizard.

Because they are bright green at hatching, the babies of the Mexican spiny-tailed iguana and the black spiny-tailed iguanas (*C. pectinata* and *C. similis* respectively) are occasionally sold as "baby green igua-

The chuckwalla, Sauromalus ater, was once a food item for Native Americans in the western states.

nas." Babies of the single dwarfed spiny-tail now available (*C. quinque-carinata*) are very like the adults in color.

Diet: Although they may be quite feisty, once acclimated, the various spiny-tailed iguanas are hardy captives. These lizards are somewhat more insectivorous, especially when young, than the green iguana. Although older texts have suggested a diet of approximately 60 percent (juveniles) to 75 percent (adults) vegetation, an even greater percentage of vegetation may prove better for the lizards.

Caging: Caging suitable for the larger spiny-tailed iguanas is identical to that provided the green iguana (see Chapter Seven). Caging used for the more diminutive forms can, of course, be considerably smaller. Still, spiny-tails of all species are quick, active creatures that enjoy room to dart about, and ample areas of seclusion. This should always be

taken into consideration when you are planning caging.

Handling: Unless acquired as babies, and worked with diligently, spiny-tailed iguanas often resist attempts to tame them. Indeed, even when a concerted effort is made to tame them, some retain an alert attitude and are neither easily handled nor, in some cases, even approached. As would be expected, this is especially true of wild-collected adults. Captive-bred spiny-tails, which are not often available in America, although often more expensive, are also usually more tolerant of human contact. German and Swiss hobbyists seem especially intrigued by these interesting iguanas, and it is from these countries that most captive-hatched babies are exported to America.

Breeding: The males of most of the larger *Ctenosaurs* have a fairly well-developed crest of vertebral scales. This is often most prominent on the nape. The crest of the adult females is lower and less noticeable. The crests of certain of the smaller forms may consist of little more than a ridge of slightly enlarged scales.

Babies are especially difficult to sex by external means; however, probing is quite conclusive, with males probing at least twice as deep as females.

All spiny-tails are oviparous. The size of the clutches may number as few as one egg in young female Yucatan spiny-tails (see next page), or occasionally to 50-plus in some old females of the larger species.

Climatic conditions, including photoperiod, relative humidity, and actual rainfall, induce breeding. Gravid female spiny-tails dig deep nesting chambers in which to place their eggs. Where suitable nesting

The black spiny-tailed iguana has become established in Florida. This one suns in Dade County.

sites are minimal, spiny-tails are known to nest communally, and have even nested with great green iguanas in Costa Rica. In rocky areas, nesting burrows may be short and angle beneath surface boulders. However, in open areas nesting burrows may near, or even slightly exceed, a yard in length.

Although it is rarely seen in captivity, the tiny Yucatan spiny-tail, *Ctenosaura defensor*, is a coveted form. It is a beautiful little lizard that is usually less than a foot (30 cm) in total length. Adult males in breeding color are clad in scales of gray, black, and cobalt and have a blanket of terra-cotta over most of their dorsum. The females and juveniles are both smaller and less brilliantly colored.

A long-term captive male Mexican spiny-tailed iguana. If it were breeding season, his body would bear an orange flush.

Rock Iguanas

The big, terrestrial rock iguanas have never been as popular with herpetoculturists as their inexpensive and readily available green cousin. Most of the species of rock iguanas are of federally endangered or threatened status and require government permits to be marketed legally in interstate commerce.

It is the rhinoceros iguana, *Cyclura c. cornuta*, a nonendangered, but still quite expensive, species that is most frequently encountered in the American pet trade. It is often referred to as the "rhino iguana."

Diet: Although it is true that in the wild, rhinoceros iguanas are opportunistic feeders, they are still predominantly vegetarian. Long-term studies have disclosed that they thrive best

and live longest (22 years or more) on vegetarian diets. Leafy greens and grated yellow vegetables now form the basic diets in the most successful breeding facilities. To this is added some fruit and a very occasional meal of water-softened, low-fat, high-quality dog food. A few insects may also be offered from time to time.

Caging: Rhino iguanas must be provided with a great deal of space. For a pair or trio of adults, a ground space of no less than 100 square feet (9 m^2) with sturdy climbing limbs is recommended. While being raised, several young may be maintained in a space half that size, but they must be watched to make sure that any emerging patterns of dominance by some do not debilitate any of their cagemates.

Rhino iguanas can become very tame, and will leave their comfortable perch in a cage and walk up to a human for a head-rub. This is a young rhino.

Handling: Adult male rhinoceros iguanas are immensely powerful lizards of bulldog-like mien. They have a cobalt-blue lining to the mouth, which is best observed from an arm's-length distance. The smaller females are somewhat less spectacular. Although all must be treated with respect, some specimens become remarkably docile—even "tame" in the broadest sense of the word. For many years The International Iguana Society had an adult male rhinoceros iguana that was so tame that it allowed all manner of overtures, even by toddlers. This should best be considered the exception, not the rule, and we recommend that discretion and care be used when handling or working with these lizards. The disposition of each lizard must be individually assessed.

Behavior: In the wild, rhinoceros iguanas are inveterate sun worshipers. Choosing a vantage point from which a wide range of vision is possible, these lizards will bask for long periods. Their dark body colors assure that they will be quickly warmed to their optimum operating temperatures by the sun, after which they forage, then bask again.

Rhinoceros iguanas are territorial lizards. This is most apparent with adult males during the breeding season. Strangely, when the lizards are immature, it is the females that are more aggressive. When juveniles of either sex are housed together, it is best to have a cage into which visual barriers have been incorporated. These can be in the form of strategically placed logs, rocks, or even partial panels of plywood or opaque plastic. A suitably warmed, preferably elevated vantage point for each specimen should be included. Rhino iguanas seem to truly enjoy utilizing piles of rocks for such observation stations.

Young rhino iguanas are more easily debilitated than adults by cool temperatures. It is suggested that smaller specimens not be subjected to temperatures of less than 60°F (16°C). Adults can drop occasionally to 50°F (10°C), and if healthy, not be harmed. Although a daytime high of 95°F (35°C) would be best when it is sunny, these large iguanas are able to thermoregulate effectively at cooler temperatures. Body temperatures of adult wild (and captive) rock iguanas, taken through cloacal readings, have registered as high as 106°F (41°C). At these temperatures the specimens are alert and quick.

Breeding: As with green iguanas, photoperiod and other climatic conditions induce breeding activities (see Chapter Ten for an overview). It is not unusual for females to begin several false nests before choosing the final site.

Once a suitable area is found, a nesting burrow of up to 3½ feet (1.1 m) in length may be dug. Barely moistened sand areas seem readily chosen. Clutches vary widely in size with the age and size of the female being important determinants. The eggs are proportionately large. Clutches numbering as few as three to more than twenty have been recorded. At a temperature of 86°F (30°C), the incubation period averages 88 days.

It is often not until several days subsequent to hatching that the neonates accept their first meal. Their diet should be similar in content to, but more finely diced than, that of the adult iguanas (see Chapter Eight for basic dietary suggestions and vitamin-mineral additives). Insufficient calcium can result in death.

Although the sexing of adult rhinoceros iguanas is not at all difficult, attempting to sex juveniles by visible means can prove challenging. It is better to rely on probing. Males probe more than twice as deep than the females. Although not difficult, if attempted with a probe of incorrect size, or done roughly or with too much pressure, injury to the iguana can occur. Probing needs to be very carefully done, or left to the experts.

Chapter Seven

Caging of Giant Green Iguanas

Baby giant green iguanas are easily—deceptively easily—caged. They really can be initially housed in a cage the size of a 15-gallon (57 L) aquarium, but we suggest that the first cage be at least twice that volume. The fact is that, if properly cared for, that pretty little 10-inch-long (25 cm) lizard that you're starting off with will not remain a baby for long. Within a couple of months, a larger cage will be needed, in a couple of more months, an even larger one, and so on.

All too often we have heard pet store personnel tell interested clients that "Yes, the iguana starter kit—usually a 10- or 15-gallon (38 or 57 L) aquarium, top, aquarium light, aspen shavings or bark nuggets, water bowl, and prepack dry iguana food—will suffice for the little green lizard," and never elucidate further. It would be better if the client were told that when it is an adult, a male green iguana is an active, agile, potentially aggressive lizard that may measure more than 6 feet (1.8 m) in length, will require a cage the size of a room, should have a source of ultraviolet A and UV-B, and that a varied diet is probably a better choice for the lizards! A female may reach only 3½ feet (1.1 m) in length and be slightly more tractable, but her caging requirements may still be a surprise for an unsuspecting, and unprepared, owner.

Caging Needs

Your iguana's caging, no matter what the lizard's size might be, needs to have:
• Physical space for the lizard.
• One or two basking limbs.
• A light/heat source and a nighttime heat source set on thermostats and timers.
• Untippable food and water bowls.
• A "dunk" watering dish large enough for the lizard to at least immerse its body.
• Ventilation.
• A "visually secure" area where your lizard can rest and look out.
• An absorbent area where defecated material will dry out and can be easily removed.

Caging styles can vary, and will depend on the climate where you live, the space you can allot for your iguana, and the caging materials that

Your cage needs to provide room to roam, room to stretch out, access to UVA and UVB light, and a ready supply of fresh food. All these are available to this green iguana, "livin' large" on the banks of the Amazon River in Iquitos, Peru.

are easiest for you to work with. If you live in a warm climate, like the southernmost half of the southern tier of states, an open wire mesh or wire panel cage may be used for at least part of the year. One particularly enterprising person has placed on the Internet her innovative design for a low-cost, knock-down iguana cage using PVC piping and joints, plastic wire ties, and coated rabbit wire.

If you live in a temperate area, a solid cage is better for your iguana. A cage with solid sides and top has different advantages than a wire cage. In both cases, with a little advance planning, the cage can be designed in easy-to-screw-together panels. This means you can add panels to make the cage larger, or you can take the cage apart and take it with you when you move.

An aquarium is one style of the solid cage that will work for the first few months you have your hatchling. The wire screen mesh top pro-

vides a convenient—and safe for the iguana—place for the basking and fluorescent lights. With a tube of Silastic, you can secure basking limbs and perching shelves, and paper towels are a fine absorbent substrate for hatchlings.

Substrate

For substrate, you need to use something that absorbs moisture, but can't be accidentally eaten by the iguanas if they lean down to pick up uneaten food. Newspaper works fine for small iguanas. The newspaper isn't particularly absorbent, so you'll need to take care when dealing with a particularly messy stool. If you simply put another sheet of newspaper over any spills or wet places, and roll the newspaper up, bending over the sides of the papers as you roll, most messes can be easily contained.

Here are some substrate choices, bad and good, in short:
• Newspaper—not very absorbent but cost-effective and readily at hand.

• Mulch—cypress, never cedar (cedar mulch contains phenols, which smell pleasant to humans but are deadly to reptiles).

• Gravel—nonabsorbent and far too easily ingested when food is placed on it.

• Indoor/outdoor carpet—gives good traction but needs to be scrubbed clean at least weekly.

• Wire mesh cage bottom or as a shelf—no chance of ingestion, but chopped vegetables or small bits of food will fall through it.

• Sand—absorbent but very messy; food clings to it; iguana can get wet and crawl through it and get covered by sand; real danger of intestinal impaction.

Cypress mulch is a good substrate choice. We like it because it is absorbent and helps mask any odors, but we also feed our iguanas from a dish placed on some flat pieces of shale. Any pieces of food pushed out of the food dish end up on the shale and can be picked up, either by us or by the iguana.

Cage Requirements

Size: Whatever style of caging you start out with, try to place the cage at least at waist level. Your iguana is an arboreal lizard, and it will enjoy looking down on things. The cage will also be easier to clean.

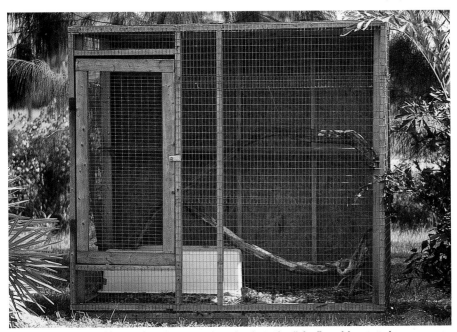

An outdoor cage is essentially permanent and solves the "size" problem—unless you add another iguana.

If you do decide to use an aquarium for your baby iguana initially, the length of the cage should always be at least twice the length of your iguana. The width must be at least as wide as the total length of your iguana, and the height should be about the length of the iguana.

The aquarium will need to be replaced as your iguana grows. In the wild, hatchling iguanas grow about 0.25 mm a day, which transposes to about a third of an inch a month. In captivity, with correct nutrition and secure caging, the growth rate is much faster. A 10-inch-long (25 cm) hatchling will be 24 inches (61 cm) long within the first year. When adult, your iguana will need a cage at least 4 feet (122 cm) wide by 6 feet (183 cm) high by 8 feet (244 cm) long. Proper lighting, temperature (see Lighting and Heating, pages 86–87), humidity, water availability, and cleanliness of substrate, perch, and glass must be always maintained.

Perches: The cage must be provided with one or more elevated perches that are at least the diameter of your lizard's body and the perches must be increased in diameter as your lizard grows (see Perches, page 83).

Building your own: Ideal iguana cages are actually rather easy to plan and construct, but the materials can be expensive and the placing of the cage can be problematic. You will save money and time if you think big, building the facility your lizard will need as an adult rather than simply adjusting the size upwards with every 6 inches (15 cm) of lizard growth. While some owners will balk at the thought of providing a cage that costs several hundred to several thousand dollars for what was initially a $25 lizard, other owners become so imbued with the project that they simply never stop planning and improving.

Outdoor cages: In the deep South, where temperatures are consistently warm and the humidity high for two-thirds of the year, large outdoor cages may be made for tame iguanas from smooth welded wire. In southern Florida or southern Texas, such a cage will quite probably suffice for your lizard year-round. These cages may also be used during suitably warm weather even at northern latitudes. However, in the North, the colder weather means that brightly illuminated, indoor, draft-free caging that will retain warmth and hold humidity must be provided. If you have access to the outdoors, there

Advantages of Wire Mesh and Solid Tanks

Wire Mesh Tanks—Advantages
• Easy and relatively inexpensive to make.
• Provide plenty of ventilation.
• Are fairly lightweight.
• Can be put outdoors in a semi-shaded area if space permits.
• Branches, food/water dishes and lights can be easily fastened in place.
• If the bottom is mesh, the feces and urates fall through to newspaper below or onto the ground.
• If the bottom is solid, absorbent paper can be put on the cage bottom for fairly easy cleanup.

Wire Mesh Tanks—Disadvantage
• Cannot be heated adequately if the weather turns chilly—70°F (21°C) or lower.

Solid Cages—Advantages
• The solid sides and top make it much easier to warm.
• Ventilation grids, ideally placed at opposite heights and in opposite corners, will allow adequate air circulation if they are large enough.

Solid Cages—Disadvantages
• If the ventilation grids don't provide enough circulation, a small exhaust fan placed near a ventilation panel will be needed to keep the air circulating in the cage.
• Basking lights will need to be fastened near the top of the cage, next to the basking area, and covered with wire mesh to avoid burns.
• Heavier than a wire cage and will take more time to clean.

are two ways you can go on this one: You can simply build a moveable cage, and take it outdoors when weather permits and move it indoors during colder weather, or you can have two cages, one outdoors and one indoors. Without outdoor access, your indoor caging needs to provide eveything your iguana needs.

Types of Caging

Wood and Wire Mesh Cages

An active adult iguana should be provided with an enclosure having a floor space of at least 4 × 8 feet (122 × 244 cm), although 6 × 10 feet (183 × 305 cm) would be better. A height of between 6 and 8 feet (183 and 244 cm), the ceiling height on most of today's houses, is suggested. The cage should be provided with:
• tree trunks and climbing limbs
• elevated shelves
• access to natural sunlight or a bank of UV-producing lights
• a hotspot for basking
• areas of seclusion
• an adequate supply of clean water.

Some owners provide a small water dish for drinking and a larger basin for bathing, and clean both as needed.

A simple cage begins with a framework of wooden 2 × 2s or 2 × 4s. The components of the frame should be nailed or screwed together. Using a screw bit on your electric drill will make the construction process much faster.

Wire mesh: This should be firmly stapled to the outside of the framework. Mesh size can be quarter-inch (6.4 mm) or larger. Half-inch (13 mm) welded wire mesh would work for both baby and large iguanas. If a smooth welded mesh or a plastic-covered wire is used, it will help pre-

vent the lizard from abrading its nose if it tries to escape. When housing a lizard as strong as an adult iguana, besides suitably strong wire (12-gauge for the wire panels), "hammer-in" wire staples, rather than those from a small staple gun, are suggested.

Door: Be sure the cage door is large enough for you to reach the bottom of the cage to clean it, or add a second door near the bottom of the cage for this purpose.

Bottom: The bottom can be a piece of plywood (¾-inch [19 mm] thickness is best, but ½-inch [13 mm] will do), or it can be wire mesh if the cage sits on a bed of newspaper.

Casters properly affixed to the wooden bottom will allow you to move the cage easily. If you have an outside deck or porch and intend to move the cage outside during good weather, be sure that whatever length you choose to make the cage, at its widest and tallest dimensions the cage is at least 2 inches (5 cm) narrower and 2 inches shorter, including caster height, than the dimensions of your deck door. The larger the casters you use, the easier it will be to move the cage.

Wire Mesh Panel Cages

Cages for large lizards can be easily made from sheets of welded 16-gauge wire panels. Panels come in 27-inch and 36-inch (69 and 91 cm) widths, and in 6-foot (183 cm)

A pet store iguana cage, rolled outside for the sun. This is good temporary housing.

lengths. Depending on the desired cage size, the panels may be used as is, trimmed, or carefully bent into the best shape and desired dimensions, then joined with small flat metal brads called "J-clamps." These very strong joiners are easily crimped with special pliers that are sold specifically for that purpose. You can also staple these panels to wooden frames made of 2 × 2s, and use metal fastening strips to assemble the panels into a cage. The cut-off lengths of the panels make good iguana ladders from one branch or shelf to another.

The panels best suited for this application are 8- to 12-gauge and have openings either ½ × 1 inch (13 × 25 m), or ½ × 2 inches (13 × 51 m), in size. The wire, the clamps, and the crimping tool are sold in hardware and feed stores.

An advantage of all-wire cages is that they are lighter than those framed of wood. We have made both permanent (unmovable) and movable cages—up to 8 feet long × 6 feet high and 4 feet wide (244 × 183 × 122 cm)—in this manner. The movable cages are placed either on a wooden frame or on top of a suitably sized sheet of plywood to which casters have been attached. Or, depending on the weight of the cage furniture, and if you have some help, you can carry the cage outside.

Solid Cages

You can make solid cages yourself, have them made, or buy a commercial model.

Although this cage used a roll of standard welded mesh for the sides, you could use the 16-guage "rabbit cage" panels to simplify construction.

Use at least ⅝-inch (16 mm) plywood if you decide to make your cage. Decide the dimensions you want; a cage that is 4 ×8 ×6 feet (122 ×244 ×183 cm) can use standard sheets of plywood, reducing both the number of cuts you have to make and the wasted wood.

Escaping: Although some iguanas will tame quickly and will seldom if ever attempt to escape their cage, others may persistently abrade their snouts in their efforts to get out. This is especially so in cages that do not contain sufficient crisscrosses of limbs and other visual barriers.

Remember, these are climbing lizards whose response to trouble, captivity, or you is to climb. Initially, watch any lizards that you place in these cages to be sure they are not injuring themselves. If they are, the iguanas will need either to be removed or their cage suitably renovated. Temporarily placing an opaque barrier such as a blanket or sheets of newspaper along the full length of the lower walls to limit visibility may deter your iguana from making escape attempts.

The Iguana Room

Some iguanas become so much a part of the family that they are given their own dedicated room. This is an excellent solution to the space problem. It is, of course, mandatory that suitable cage furniture, water receptacles, heating, and lighting are provided and that all are properly secured. It is a good idea to cover wooden floors with a sheet of linoleum to prevent staining and other damage.

Some owners prefer to allow tame iguanas to roam the entire house. Your iguana will usually soon find a preferred basking area; direct it to where you wish it to be by providing a sturdy, elevated, warmed, and illuminated perch. An area such as in front of a sunny picture window is usually ideal. Carpeted cat jungle gyms, kitty trees, or free-form macaw and parrot stands of varying sizes can be used either in a cage or merely placed near a sunny window in a room. These may consist of several platforms, sizable limbs, and other climbing and resting surfaces, all of which will be readily accepted by iguanas. Again, you must be sure there is nothing on which your iguana can harm itself but most of these "playgrounds" are fully suitable. Some carpet styles may snag an iguana's toenails, an often overlooked potential problem that could result in torn claws, broken toes, or even a broken limb. Artificial lighting, which also should provide heating, can be directed toward the topmost platform.

Be sure to take the following precautions:
• Be certain that all toilets are closed, that all house plants are nontoxic, that all windows are either closed or have heavy wire over the screens—the claws of a large iguana can tear through many window screens—that curtains or draperies can withstand the onslaught of 20 sturdy, recurved claws, and that all closet doors and

entryways to forbidden areas are tightly closed.

• Make sure that doors on return springs cannot inadvertently slam closed on your iguana.

• Be sure fireplaces are screened and chimney flues are closed, and that breakable items cannot be pushed from shelves. In other words, any rooms or other accessible areas must be fully pet iguana-proofed.

• Be sure that your visitors know about your iguana, and give serious thought to simply restricting your iguana to a single, unused room when you have company. Even a relative can become very angry and upset when frightened by an iguana.

• A lamp or other electrical appliance, when knocked over by a prowling iguana, can create a fire hazard. This is a very serious danger if no one is at home.

Greenhouses

Greenhouses of innumerable styles and materials are readily available today. These vary from simple, self-standing, fully constructed units from shed dealers, through myriad do-it-yourself kits, to elaborate and decorative commercial kinds that may be either self-standing or of an attractive add-on design that will provide your iguana with a wonderfully spacious cage and you with a new room. We removed an exterior wall from our house and had an add-on greenhouse installed. Unless you are very handy, these latter greenhouse types are best left to a contractor to set up. Greenhouses are usually considered

Heat lamps are good, but they should be shielded to prevent burns, should the iguana figure out a way to come into contact with the light.

permanent structures, and in many communities a building permit is required to install one legally.

Security: If your greenhouse is self-standing and separated from your house, absolute security is essential. To this end, after seeing exactly how fast a startled iguana can move, many people using such a facility have installed double entrance doors separated by a distance of several feet. Additionally, all heating and cooling units, and all bulbs that emit heat must be entirely screened from the inside to prevent injury to and the escape of your iguana inhabitants.

Base: We further suggest that the base of the unit either be flush upon a concrete slab, affixed on top of a concrete or brick wall, or be sunk a

foot (30 cm) or more below the surface of the ground. This will preclude easy access by outside predatory creatures such as dogs, cats, raccoons, skunks, or even rats and mice, and a tunnel for escape by your lizards.

Double glazing: In all cases, double glazing should be employed as an energy-saving option, especially in regions subject to extreme cold or heat, and such a thermal barrier may actually be required by some building codes if the greenhouse becomes a part of your home. Double glazing just makes it easier for you to control the temperatures in the greenhouse, and your greenhouse more comfortable for the user, whether two- or four-legged.

Plantings: It is important to provide the appropriate plantings, watering, heating and lighting systems, and cage furniture. The possi-

bility, and feasibility, of providing a small pond and waterfall, often much-wanted accouterments in low-humidity areas, should be well thought out at the outset. Plantings must be nonnoxious as well as sturdy enough to withstand the body weight of, and an occasional tasting by, your iguana. Sansevieria are ideal accent plantings, and although needing high-light situations, hibiscus bushes should be considered both for a perch and for your iguana to nibble on. Ficus (tropical figs) of various types, but especially *Ficus benjamina*, are also inexpensive, sturdy, and easily grown.

When approached with imagination and forethought, the interior of even a small greenhouse can become both the focal point of your home and a wonderful home for your giant green iguana.

Cage Furniture for Your Iguana

When purchasing your baby iguana, and especially when considering the iguana cage that will eventually be needed to house the lizard when adult, remember your iguana is an arboreal lizard. A caged iguana will often climb to the very top of its wire-sided cage, and attempt to rest while clinging uncomfortaly to the uppermost cage wire. An iguana caged in a glass-sided cage may try continuously and fruitlessly to climb the unscalable vertical glass that sur-

rounds it. It is for this reason that we advocate vertically oriented cages with ample, easily climbable logs or shelves, horizontal, or gently inclined, elevated perches.

Perches

Perches and other cage furniture can serve two purposes: adding to the desired cage acceptability by the iguana, and to the lizard's psychological well-being by providing visual barriers.

Any elevated perch that is provided for your iguana should be sturdily anchored and suitably substantial. Although hatchling iguanas weigh so little that they can easily perch on a slender twig, an adult iguana can weigh several pounds and will need correspondingly heavier limbs. Great green iguanas often sprawl while basking, drooping their legs and part of their tails over the sides of their perch. We suggest that you always provide your iguana with a basking branch that is at least the diameter of its body, and preferably one and a half times its diameter. The perch(es) must be securely affixed to prevent toppling. Since iguanas prefer to thermoregulate on an elevated perch, direct the warming beams of the UVA/UVB light onto this perch from above. Be certain to position the light so your iguana cannot burn itself.

Cleaning the perch: In the wild, tropical rains keep the arboreal perches of iguanas washed clean. Unless your cage is outside where the same cleansing can occur, you'll need to wash and sterilize facilities and furniture. A weak chlorine bleach solution may be used for this purpose, but you should then rinse

No matter how good (or how bad) your caging, take your iguana out of the cage and handle it every day or two. This makes handling less stressful for both of you in the long run.

Flat, wide shelving works well for the larger, more terrestrial iguanas, such as this rhino iguana.

or spray off all washed items thoroughly. Iguanas are tolerant of chlorine-based cleansers, but are not tolerant of phenol-based (often listed as "pine-scented") home cleaners.

Heat Sources

Although hot rocks are almost universally available and often suggested, we consider these a very unnatural heat source for iguanas. Iguanas are physiologically, and psychologically, adapted for warming their bodies from the top down. In nature, this is accomplished by orienting and changing their body positions in relation to the warmth provided by, and the position of, the sun. Warming solely, or even primarily, from the belly up, such as on top of a hot rock, is unnatural and if the rock happens to be overly warm, can actually be dangerous. Heat-induced trauma to internal organs, as well as egg damage to gravid (pregnant) females can be caused by prolonged basking on an over-warmed hot rock. Also, with their primitive nervous system, serious thermal burns can actually be sustained by your iguana before the lizard is aware of the problem. These warnings should not be construed as meaning that a very cold perch is better for your iguana; this is not at all the case. We are simply advocating that ventral heating be very carefully monitored and used primarily in conjunction with, not in place of, above-cage lighting and heating.

Hidebox

Many reptiles benefit from a hidebox. A tame iguana might find a hidebox useful, as may an iguana that you never hope to tame; however, providing the security of a hidebox can be of questionable value to an iguana that is in the process of being tamed. If your lizard can conceal itself every time you approach, and needs to be forcefully removed from its hidebox, it may never tame as thoroughly as you would like.

Hideboxes in outside cages have another benefit on days that are marginally too cool for your iguana. They can be fitted with a heat lamp, taking care that the iguana cannot burn itself, and are more easily temperature-regulated than the entire cage. We use large heating pads called "hog blankets" on part of the floor of the hidebox. However, in marginal weather, you must either restrict your iguana to its hidebox, or carefully check that it does not wander out into its cage and become numbed by the cold.

Greenery

There is no question that plants provide beauty and humidity to an iguana cage, and because of the visual barriers they offer, accent plants will also provide "Iggy" with an enhanced sense of security. But at no time when you are considering or choosing greenery can you lose sight of the fact that your iguana is an herbivorous lizard that will sample every plant with which it comes in contact. Choose plants wisely; choose only plants that are known to have entirely benign properties. A tame iguana biting into a very acrid plant may sample it once and never again. If the plant is acrid but not toxic, little damage will be done, but if the plant does contain harmful alkaloids or have other dangerous properties, sickness, injury, or even death of your iguana may follow.

Houseplants: The properties of many commonly offered houseplants are entirely unknown. The properties of other plants touted as dangerously toxic may, in fact, be toxic to mammals, but entirely benign to herbivorous reptiles. Some such plants would be many of the various philodendrons and, perhaps, the too-maligned poinsettia. In many cases, we simply don't know, so it will be up to you to choose plants prudently.

Sometimes a plant doesn't need to actually be toxic to be harmful to the health of a lizard that eats it. Two such examples would be spinach—not that you would probably be growing spinach in an iguana's cage anyway—and the pretty little potted plant known as wood sorrel (*Oxalis* sp.). Because the oxalic acid that these and related plants contain will bind to and render calcium unusable, avoid using them.

We have allowed our iguanas unfettered access to the Asian fig known as *Ficus benjamina* and hibiscus. The lizards seem most inclined to ignore the foliage of the former, but will eat blossoms and leaves of the latter. It is important that if you use greenhouse plants, no insecticides, either contact or systemic, or fertilizers are present.

Plastic plants: Many people decorate their iguana enclosures with plastic plants. Iguanas generally test the edibility of these with their tongues, then lose interest.

Toys: You can also use prepackaged vines, rope nets and hammocks, climbing ropes, and many other kinds of cage furniture that are commercially available. All probably have their applications, but care

should be used with all that there are no loose ends or other hazards that could harm your iguana. These "toys" will need to be removed, washed, and disinfected periodically. They should be completely dry before replacing them.

Lighting and Heating

The Role of Full-spectrum Lighting

Natural unfiltered sunlight is, of course, the ultimate in full-spectrum lighting. It provides, among other wavelengths, both ultraviolet (UV) and infrared; normal window glass does not allow the passage of most UV. It is ultraviolet—especially UVA and UVB—that seems to be of particular importance to our iguanas.

Researchers agree that UVA in sufficient amounts permits the "natural" manufacture—the synthesizing—of vitamin D, and in particular vitamin D_3, by an iguana. In turn, D_3 allows the proper metabolizing of calcium. When an iguana has unfettered access to natural sunlight and is fed at least a reasonably good diet, fewer D_3-calcium dietary additives are needed.

Researchers further agree that UVB promotes the natural behavior of an iguana. Thus, if your iguana does not have access to natural unfiltered sunlight, a full-spectrum (UV-emitting) bulb provides a very real benefit to the lizard. Since artificial lighting does not produce as much UV as natural sunlight, it is suggested that iguanas so provided be given some D_3-calcium dietary supplements.

Types of Bulbs

Traditionally, the most effective production of UVA and UVB has been by several brands of fluorescent bulbs. Perhaps the best known of these was Vita-lite. Fluorescent bulbs produce comparatively little heat, and severe thermal burns to lizards, even in almost direct contact, seldom occur. However, when fluorescent bulbs are used, there is usually an additional necessity to provide above-cage heat by using one or more incandescent bulbs.

A full-spectrum mercury vapor bulb that also produces heat and that uses a standard incandescent socket is available. We use this and have been favorably impressed by the reactions of the lizards. We have found that our iguanas, as well as other lizards and turtles, preferentially bask beneath them, abandoning other well-established basking areas lit and heated by other methods. Our UVA/UVB bulbs are positioned so that they heat a well-elevated perch to a temperature of 95 to 98°F (35–36.7°C), measured on the top of the basking limb, but are separated from the lizards by the wire top of the cage.

This degree of warmth allows the lizard to attain the 89 to 95°F (31.7–35°C) body temperature that best suits it. It is at this temperature that your iguana is the most disease-resistant, and bodily functions are optimum. Your iguana will behave normally only when a combination of brilliant full-spectrum illumination and heat is provided. Either, without the other, is not sufficient.

Can an iguana be kept successfully without this special full-spectrum lighting? Yes, but why would you choose this sort of life for your iguana? Iguanas deprived of UVA/UVB lighting seem invariably to need considerable amounts of dietary D_3-calcium. The actual effectiveness of the gut absorption of these additives is a topic of current debate.

City Iguanas and Sunlight

The UVA and UVB wavelengths induce natural behavior (UVA) and allow the synthesis of vitamin D (UVB) in the skin. Without vitamin D, especially vitamin D_3, it is not possible for your iguana to metabolize sufficient calcium through its gut lining to maintain the necessary amounts in the blood. In turn, when the blood-calcium level drops abnormally, calcium is removed from the bones to maintain a minimum blood level. This becomes the culprit behind metabolic bone disease (MBD). Although vitamin D_3 can be provided as a dietary supplement, how well that oral vitamin can be utilized is still unknown.

Can there be too much of a good thing? Can your lizard overdose on full-spectrum lighting—especially nat-

might, in fact, be as much an effort to regulate the intake of UV light as to prevent overheating. However, periodically throughout the day, for varying durations, iguanas usually emerge from the cover of the foliage to bask in exposed positions, again, perhaps for thermoregulation, but during which time a greater intake of UV certainly occurs.

We urge that if your iguana is kept outside, you provide a shaded area where it can escape the rays of the sun should it choose to.

For most of us, it is not how to protect the lizards from the unfiltered sunlight that plagues us, but rather how to get the lizard into unfiltered sunlight at all. Providing sunlight can be a special problem for apartment dwellers and for others who live in the northern states.

We suggest two items—there are probably many more—that may help alleviate the problem:

1. A firmly affixed, protruding window box cage that becomes accessible to your uncaged iguana on warm days when your window is opened. When located on the sunny side of your home—usually the south or the west side—this can often offer several hours of unfiltered sunlight to your iguana each day, during suitably warm weather. Because even moderate heat can reflect from walls and

ural unfiltered sunlight? The truth is that we are not sure. Certainly, after an exposed early morning period of thermoregulation, wild iguanas often seek shelter beneath the leaves of their home tree.

In Miami, the big lizards clamber well back into the interior of the very densely foliated clumps of Brazilian pepper they often frequent. This windows and intensify to lethal temperatures, never confine your iguana in the sunning. Remember also that the claws of even a moderate-size iguana can easily tear through all commonly used window screening. We suggest that nothing less durable than ⅛-inch (3.2 mm) welded mesh hardware cloth be used on all sides of the sunning cage. Used prudently, this window box arrangement can be of great benefit to your lizard.

2. The second method is easier yet, and provides the possibility of additional interactions between iguana and people. This is the iguana harness and leash, a simple contraption made of a single piece of soft but very sturdy nylon, a metal clasp, and a metal clip. When fed properly through the clasp, the leash falls into two loops. The first of these fits snugly around the iguana's neck; the second fits equally snugly around the lizard's torso immediately behind the forelimbs, then clips to itself above the lizard's back.

Although all iguanas can be restrained on these harness-leash arrangements, not all are comfortable on them. These restraints are suited best for smaller, thoroughly tame iguanas that are not easily startled. Each time we place our moderately tame male iguana on a leash, he will roll so persistently on his long axis that the entire leash is rolled tightly around his body. He is not hurt by doing this, and the leash is easily unrolled, but it is a reaction that we had not expected from him. After being on the leash for a minute or two, the iguana calms down and begins either to bask or to investigate his new surroundings.

These leashes can be used anywhere that it is legal to have an iguana, and can provide a tame lizard an opportunity to sun even on the sunny front stoop of a yardless brownstone. But don't leave your iguana unattended.

D₃ and Calcium

Vitamin D_3, often referred to as cholecalciferol by veterinarians and dietary researchers, is the key that allows your iguana to metabolize calcium. Your iguana can make its own cholecalciferol if provided UVA in natural unfiltered sunlight, or full-spectrum lighting having a chromatic index of 90 or greater (Frye, 1997). You can supply it in a dietary supplement, which is termed preformed cholecalciferol.

Simply stated, if too little cholecalciferol is present, your iguana cannot use calcium, even when the latter is present in ample amounts. When insufficient blood calcium is present, your iguana's parathyroid glands will take calcium from the bones to maintain the levels in the blood. If uncorrected within a reasonable amount of time, metabolic bone disease will result.

If an excess of preformed (dietary) cholecalciferol is given to the iguana, it is possible for it to become hypercalcemic (develop calcium deposits in muscle tissue). This condition will not occur when full-spectrum lighting is employed to induce self-made or endogenous cholecalciferol.

Despite arguments to the contrary by some researchers, Dr. Frederic Frye, a comparative veterinary pathologist, feels that excess preformed cholecalciferol is absorbed by the digestive system of iguanas. He has found soft tissue deposits typical of hypercholecalciferolemia in necropsied iguanas.

Hypercalcemia is difficult to diagnose in iguanas. It may be suspected if your iguana begins acting "differently" and is being fed such cholecalciferol-rich (and not recommended) items as monkey chow, dog food, or cat food.

A proper diet, full-spectrum lighting, and prudent use of dietary D_3-calcium supplements will assure that your iguana does not under- or overdose on these important elements.

To sum up:
• Full-spectrum lighting is our method of choice for providing D_3.
• Iguanas can metabolize dietary D_3-calcium.
• Dietary supplementation of D_3 has been rather firmly implicated in the overmetabolizing of calcium.
• There is no real formula that can be offered to assure the safety of your iguanas when dietary supplements are used.
• Common sense dictates that more D_3-calcium can be metabolized safely by fast-growing baby iguanas and by ovulating females about to lay down eggshells.

If, despite your prudence, your iguana shows signs of either metabolic bone disease or hypercalcemia, seek veterinary assessment and assistance. For more on diets, see Chapter Eight.

Iguana Cagemates

The question, "Can I keep other lizards with my iguana?" is often asked by iguana keepers. Quite honestly, there is no simple answer to this question. We often do keep at least two species together, but many folks are vehemently against the mixing of species. We kept a pair of young adult Australian frilled lizards, *Chlamydosaurus kingii*, with our green iguanas. Several factors, the most important two being the size of

This young iguana, unsure of his surroundings, inflates his body to look larger.

The green water dragon is also from "the jungle"—but its jungle is Southeast Asia.

your cage and the temperament of your iguana(s), must be considered. The lizards' comparative sizes, the possibility of disease crossover, suitability of habitat, cage temperature regime, method of feeding, and compatibility of diets must also be addressed.

Baby iguanas of both sexes and most larger female iguanas will allow caging and cagemate liberties that would not be tolerated by an adult male iguana, especially an adult male in breeding readiness. Be aware, however, that the introduction of a cagemate when both it and your iguana are babies does not in any way assure that each will tolerate the other throughout their potentially long lives.

Cage Size

As would be expected, a cage housing more than a single lizard should be proportionately larger than a cage containing only one lizard, and a cage holding one or more large lizards must necessarily be larger than a cage containing a similar number of small lizards.

At the outset, you must acknowledge that when cared for properly, the 8-inch-long (20 cm) baby iguana that you are buying today will grow. So, even when kept alone, an adult iguana is a lizard that will need the largest cage that you can possibly provide, with the minimum size being 8 × 6 × 4.5 feet (244 × 183 × 137 cm). If you add more lizards, you must add correspondingly more cage size and more basking spots. It's that simple.

Note: Crowded lizards are much more apt to squabble than those with ample cage space.

Optimum Cage Temperature

An optimum daytime temperature for an iguana when on its basking limb is in the 86 to 95°F (30–35°C) range. If you decide to house a desert lizard such as a bearded dragon (*Pogona vitticeps*) with the iguana, you will need to provide a somewhat lower vantage point having a surface temperature of 120°F (48.9°C). Although providing such diverse temperatures can be easily accomplished in a large cage, it would be a daunting, if not impossible, challenge in a small container.

Cage Humidity

Iguanas enjoy high humidity. Research the humidity needs of potential cage companions. Open wire cages are often more readily adaptable to multiple humidity levels than closed cages.

Companion Lizard Species and Size

Suitable possible companions for your great green iguana will change as the size of your iguana does. Although a knight anole, *Anolis equestris*, or a Tokay gecko, *Gekko gecko*, might coexist in reasonable peace and safety with a baby or medium-sized iguana, those lizards could be injured or even eaten by an adult iguana. On the flip side of this coin, a large spiny-tailed iguana or basilisk will probably eat your baby green iguana. Comparative size at any given moment is an important consideration.

Some possible companion lizard species for a medium- to large-size great green iguana might be the following.

The larger species of spiny-tailed iguanas, *Ctenosaura* species: These are often available in pet stores, and being of neotropical origin, will tolerate a range of humidity similar to your green iguana. Spiny-tails may near or equal your green iguana in size when adult. Although they preferentially eat a greater percentage of animal protein than is considered healthy for your green iguana, spiny-tails can and will do well on a diet consisting largely of healthy vegetation. If you do provide your spiny-tail a diet high in animal protein, such as insects, pinkie mice, dog food, and so on, you must devise a way to keep this away from your green iguana. As a downside, spiny-tailed iguanas are often flighty and difficult to handle, often remaining wary and on edge when you are near the cage. This uneasiness can easily be imparted to all but the tamest of green iguanas.

The green water dragon, *Physignathus cocincinus*: This species is native to Southeast Asia and is very readily and inexpensively available in the pet trade. Most specimens available are collected from the wild and are moderately to seriously debilitated by the time they are offered for sale. If at all debilitated, green water dragons can be quite difficult to acclimate successfully and the mortality rate can be quite high. Do not consider placing a green water dragon with your iguana until the water dragon's health has been ascertained (we urge veterinary assessment for this). Like your iguana, the green water dragon

Young green water dragons look a bit like young green iguanas.

is a lizard species that prefers moderately warm temperatures—85 to 95°F (29–35°C)—climbs well, swims well, and tames rather easily. Once acclimated, water dragons allow careful handling without showing undue stress. Males are the larger sex, often exceeding a bulky 24 inches (61 cm) in total length. Although they may eat a little plant material, green water dragons are primarily insectivorous. Captives also readily consume pinkie mice. It was once thought baby mice were good for water dragons, but it is now thought that because of their high fat content, pinkies should be offered only as occasional treats. Your green iguana should not be allowed access to the insect and pinkie diet provided the water dragons.

The brown water dragon, *Physignathus leseueri*: Although less colorful than the green water dragon, this is a hardier, more temperature-tolerant species. Most available examples of this impressive lizard are captive bred and hatched, and usually not seriously parasitized or otherwise debilitated. Females and young are clad in scales of rich brown with tan to olive gray bands. Adult males, which may exceed 24 inches (61 cm) in overall length, when in breeding readiness develop a chest and anterior stomach of beautiful scarlet. This lizard species climbs and swims well, and runs rapidly. They tame readily and usually allow careful handling. Brown water dragons are primarily insectivorous, but captives will eagerly

In breeding season, male brown water dragons get brighter in color.

accept pinkie mice. Because the high fat content of pinkie mice may prove detrimental to brown water dragons over a long period of time, we suggest that you provide a diet that consists primarily of gut-loaded insects. In any case, it will be necessary to prevent your iguana access to the dragon's high animal protein diet.

The magnificent 32-inch-long (81 cm) Australian frilled lizard, *Chlamydosaurus kingii*: This is one of our favorite lizards. It is the world's only lizard species to have the trademark distensible neck frill. It is a species of the dry northern Australian and southern New Guinean woodlands. In natural habitat it is often seen clinging to the trunks of trees, on top of anthills (termite mounds), or on other vantage points. It is adept at climbing but is equally adept at running. Its bipedal dashes and stance

have been seen by millions of television viewers and moviegoers around the world; however, more often than on the ground, the frilled lizard will display while clinging vertically to the bole of a eucalypt.

Until very recently these big, hardy, agamids were seen only in zoological gardens, but they are now bred in captivity in considerable numbers. They have proven easily handleable, but need room to run.

Their colors are dark, especially when the lizards are cold. When warm, a suffusion of light brown pigment often dominates. The frill, which is narrowest beneath the throat and interrupted above the neck (nuchally) may have red, yellow, or tan and black highlights. The species is oviparous and lays from four to ten eggs. Ours consume crickets, mealworms, caterpillars, a few pinkie mice, and occasionally a few small pieces of melon or other sweet fruit. The animal matter is fed to the frillies by hand, thus keeping it from the green iguanas with which they share their cage.

The brown basilisk and the green basilisk (*Basiliscus vittatus* and *B. plumifrons*, respectively): These are both rather commonly seen pet store lizards, but because they are so nervous, we do not recommend either species of basilisk as an iguana companion.

Adult males of the green basilisk have finlike crests on the back and tail and a double crest on the head. It is from the narrow, plumelike anterior cranial crest that the vernacular of "plumed basilisk" and specific name of "plumifrons" is derived. The ground color is green, varying from light to dark, often with blue lateral spots and some vertical black markings in the vertebral crest. The iris is brilliant orange-yellow. Adult males attain a length of more than 28 inches (71 cm). Adult females are several inches smaller.

The brown basilisk is just that, brown with darker and lighter markings. It is somewhat smaller than its green relative and lacks a vertebral (back) crest.

Basilisks are inhabitants of forest pool, marsh, and swamp edges. They climb and swim well, and run bipedally. They range from Miami (introduced) and Mexico southward to Guatemala and Costa Rica. Basilisks are insectivorous, but captives will also accept an occasional pinkie mouse. Captive green basilisks tend to lose their coveted bright green coloration. Perhaps a diet high in beta-carotenes would prevent this. Should you decide to try iguanas and basilisks together, your iguanas must not be allowed access to the basilisk's insect and rodent diet.

Pond Buddies: Goldfish, Koi, Frogs

Sizable pools are often incorporated into greenhouse setups and large outside cages. It is possible to stock a few goldfish, koi, or leopard frogs in such a pool. These insect and fish food-eating inhabitants are usually completely ignored by the iguanas.

Birds

Until we visited the Santa Fe Teaching Zoo in Gainesville, Florida, we hadn't given much thought to the possibility of keeping birds with iguanas, but, provided the cage is large enough (meaning aviary-sized) and the birds are nonpredaceous, such a pleasing combination is entirely possible. The teaching zoo has such costly exotics as mousebirds and touracos caged with their iguanas, but inexpensive types such as diamond doves, turtledoves, and Java rice birds would also thrive. We would suggest that the bird-iguana cage be no less than $12 \times 8 \times 8$ feet $(3.6 \times 2.4 \times 2.4$ m) in size.

Lizard Compatibility

Great green iguanas are not considered communal lizards. They are often more aggressive toward others of their own species than toward cage companions of other types. Noncompeting body language and differing, species-specific pheromones are probably the reasons behind this.

With that said, adequate cage space is of the essence, whether keeping iguanas by themselves, or combining them with other species. If too tightly confined, not only will iguanas not thrive, but they will often be aggressive toward cage companions they would otherwise ignore.

As would be expected, iguanas that are too young to have established the need to protect a given territory usually ignore cage companions entirely. Larger iguanas, females, or nonbreeding males in adequately sized cages are also often entirely at ease with other companion species. However, fully adult males in breeding readiness can be aggressive toward any other thing that moves. The change from amiably compatible to overtly aggressive can happen literally overnight. Watch all communal cages carefully and be ready to intervene and separate if necessary.

Parasite Crossover

That wild-collected lizards harbor endoparasites is no secret. That healthy, captive-bred lizards also often harbor endoparasites is less well known. In fact, it is so difficult to entirely rid some lizards of certain endoparasites that a veterinarian may find it necessary to weigh the purging against the long-term health of the lizard. And yes, a lizard can be the very picture of health and continue to harbor a reasonable load of endoparasites. They may have problems dealing with parasites with which they have not evolved. For example, a green iguana may become rapidly debilitated by endoparasites derived from an Asian water dragon, and vice versa. It is for this reason that if you are housing various lizards together, quarantine (see page 113), fecal assessment, and treatment by a qualified reptile veterinarian, if warranted, and absolute cage cleanliness are necessary.

Suitable Habitats

When keeping any lizards communally, whether of a single or of multiple species, a suitable section of habitat must be provided for each. This may mean that more than one basking area is needed, or that one basking perch be horizontal, for your iguana, and another projects upward and slopes gently like a natural snag, for bearded dragons or frilled lizards. Water dragons will appreciate a large soaking receptacle. Bearded dragons are quite terrestrial, enjoying a large, solid floor area over which they may easily move, while frilled lizards, water dragons, spiny-tailed iguanas, and green iguanas will be entirely at home, moving easily about, in a cage with a wire bottom. It is necessary that you research and supply the needs of your lizards, rather than expect that they will adapt to whatever you choose to provide.

Subadult brown water dragons bear distinctive stripes.

Potential Feeding Problems

When feeding foliage-eating green iguanas with which insectivorous lizards are housed, this seeming non-problem can become fraught with previously unassumed complications. We have found two solutions for the need to feed each lizard type discretely. First, easiest, and least tedious is the moving of the insectivorous lizard to a separate feeding terrarium for each feeding. Secondly and more tedious, but the method we employ, the insectivorous species can be hand-fed daily. Although we made no concerted effort to tame any species, by using this interactive method of feeding, our frilled lizards have remained accustomed to our presence as they have grown from hatchlings to young adults.

And finally, no matter how serene the caging arrangement may appear, never—repeat *never*—become complacent about lizard compatibility. Lizards that have seemed fully compatible for months, or even years, may suddenly become adversarial, necessitating an immediate, and perhaps permanent, separation.

Chapter Eight

Giant Green Iguana Diets

Think of your iguana as a tree-dwelling cow, and you'll have a basic idea of what it needs for its diet. Not only do iguanas eat a foliage diet, but like cows, they intersperse eating with resting. Those given a chance to sun with long periods of inactivity spend their time digesting their high-fiber diet. They stay in trees, nibble here, nibble there, sun, rest, nibble a bit more, and rest a lot more. Several hours before sunset they return to their sleeping trees and remain there until sunrise.

In the wild, iguanas eat in short feeding bursts from late morning to early afternoon. They eat leaves, blossoms, and fruit from select herbs, shrubs, trees, and vines. Many plant species in their diet are abundant, but the lizards selectively eat the less common species and the seasonally abundant foods. Of those foods, they select young leaves, flower buds, and some fruit. Mature leaves are less often eaten.

Providing Variety

Variety in the diet is not accomplished on a daily basis, but over a period of days. Growing iguanas select foods higher in protein than older iguanas, and maintain higher body temperatures, perhaps to increase their digestive efficiency. The larger the iguana, the more efficient its metabolism, and the further it can travel between food resources. In contrast, baby iguanas are limited by their small size. They must feed more frequently, and are limited to a smaller geographical area, than the larger adults.

Since your iguana isn't kept in the leafy trees of Central America, its diet is going to be simply what you can offer, and since the new diet varies from the diet the iguanas evolved with, you'll have to strive to offer a diet that can offer the same nutrition. The good news is that we can come close enough to a natural diet to allow them to live long lives, and to provide them with nutrition that permits them to reproduce, if that's your goal.

Certainly you realize you could eat all day long yourself and still not consume the vitamins and minerals your body needs. Because you are providing a substitute diet, you'll need to add a vitamin/mineral sup-

Is it safe to eat? This young iguana displays his unease by his erect stance and puffed up body but the meal in front of him is tempting (he gave in and ate).

plement to your iguana's diet. You'll also need to provide a varied diet so your iguana won't "lock onto" a food item to the exclusion of others.

In a nutshell, provide a diet with 45 percent vegetables and 45 percent leafy greens, 5 to 15 percent fruit, and 1 to 10 percent grains— whole wheat bread or a multigrain bread would cover this one. This is not to say that each day you painstakingly offer 45 percent each of leafy greens and chopped solid vegetables; simply average the offerings out over a week or so. Feed romaine and chopped carrots one day, escarole and chopped apples another, crumbled bread and chopped turnip greens the third day, and so on. The two key words are variety—at least ten items on a rotating basis—and try almost anything.

Leafy Greens

There are a few plants that aren't good for iguanas, and a few more that can be safely offered on a limited basis. Let's start with the leafy green list. When choosing leafy vegetables, choose those that are the darkest. Turnip greens, collards, mustard greens, dandelion greens and flowers, mulberry leaves and fruit, romaine, kale, parsley, escarole, and nasturtiums (all parts) are all excellent foods. We'll include in this group rose and hibiscus blossoms, alfalfa pellets, clover leaves and blossoms, and various hays and grasses.

Bulk or solid vegetables include mung bean sprouts, beans, including leaves and stems, grated squashes, thawed frozen mixed vegetables (avoid those with broccoli, or pick it out and eat it yourself), green beans, cabbages (green or Chinese), peas, avocado, opuntia pads and yams. Chop the vegetables into small pieces; younger iguanas aren't going to swallow anything that's too big or too hard to mouth, and their gut fauna may not be well devel-

Fresh greens, squash, okra, and green beans prove irresistible to a green iguana.

oped enough to break down this tougher cellulose.

Fruit, Soybean Products, and Bread

For fruit, try chopped and mixed apples, bananas, papayas, mangos—remove the skin, just to be safe; it is toxic to humans and may or may not be toxic to iguanas—blackberries, strawberries, kiwi, tomatoes, and melons. Tofu and other soybean products are also often enjoyed by iguanas but should be fed sparingly. The breads can include unsweetened bran dry cereals and whole grain breads.

The Calcium and Phosphorus Balance

The diet you provide should be one in which the ratio of calcium to phosphorus is 1:1 or 2:1. This means that the quantity of calcium (C) is twice or three times the quantity of phosphorus (P). The vast majority of these requirements should be derived from leafy greens. Some plants appear at first blush to be ideal for green iguanas, but they contain poor Ca:P levels; broccoli is one of these, only its tiny little leaves contain a good Ca:P level. Iceberg lettuce not only has a poor Ca:P level but offers essentially no nutrition at all. Other possible food plants, such as spinach and rhubarb, contain oxalates that bind to calcium and render the latter unusable. At least the oxalates are known to bind to calcium when ingested by mammals, and it is thought that they do so in folivorous lizards, but the truth is, you could offer these plants, except iceberg lettuce, as *part* of a balanced diet.

All the suggested foods here have acceptable Ca:P levels. If you're unsure of the calcium:phosphorus content of a food plant, consult publications such as the *Composition of Foods, Handbook Number 8*, published by the USDA.

Vitamin-Mineral Supplements

Fast-growing baby iguanas and ovulating females will need calcium/D_3 supplementation at least twice weekly; half-grown to fully grown males will need it only once every week or two. It doesn't take much. A pinch sprinkled over the food will be enough, even if all the food is not eaten.

In addition to the calcium/D_3 supplements, we provide ovulating and fast-growing hatchling iguanas a multivitamin supplement twice weekly. Adult males get supplements once a week. We have used Osteoform for many years and have not observed any unwanted side effects. Again, simply sprinkle a pinch of the vitamin supplement over the food, and don't be concerned if all of it is not eaten.

Correcting an Iguana's Diet

There may come a time when you choose to adopt an iguana that has been maintained on an incorrect diet. Since it may take months, or even years, for the effects of an improper diet to be reflected in declining health, your new lizard may appear entirely normal in all respects. We adopted one bright green baby that superficially looked to be in fine shape—but he was unable to support his own weight on his legs to walk. Fortunately, he fed very readily on chopped greens mix from our grocery store.

Ideally, your iguana would just begin eating the new diet when you presented it, but that is not usually the case. Iguanas become very demanding about their diet, especially if they have eaten a specific item for a long period. The chances are quite good that it will be necessary to resort to trickery to effect the necessary diet change. Begin attempting, of course, by mixing the new dietary components with the old. It may be necessary to dice them and mix them thoroughly; in fact, it would probably be best to do so. Sometimes this subterfuge works. If your iguana refuses the new diet, don't worry—yet. Present fresh amounts daily. If your iguana continues to pick out only its favored items, a finer puree may make dietary high grading impossible. Iguanas will also be more apt to accept a change in diet if they are hungry—in some cases, *extremely* hungry. To add this variable to a food change, merely withhold all food for a day or up to four days, keeping in mind the size and overall condition of your lizard. (Do not use this technique on a weakened iguana. Use a slurry of Pedialyte and rabbit chow, administered by a drop-

Toxic Versus Safe Plants

Toxic Plants

Many lists of so-called toxic plants have been compiled, but keep in mind that what is toxic to humans may not be toxic to animals. Poison ivy and mushrooms known to be poisonous to humans are eaten with impunity by many creatures, as are many of the more toxic fruits of solanaceous plants (nightshades). What is fatally poisonous to one group of animals may be a delicacy to others. In the wild, reptiles probably naturally recognize potentially problematic plants by odor or by the merest taste. This may not be so when they are introduced to a new geographic area or when they are captive. Please understand, we are not advocating that you experiment with any plant of questionable safety; there are simply too many "safe" plants to have to do so. However, we are saying that not all plants thought to be toxic are necessarily fatal.

Safe Plants

Listed below are some plants that are known to be safe foods for your iguana. Besides those listed below, there are many other safe and nutritious plants. It merely means that this plant is a nontoxic (safe) food for your iguana or other herbivorous reptile. The unlimited vegetables are those you can offer for the majority of the diet; the limited quantities are those items that need to be limited to 5 to 15 percent of the diet.

Unlimited Quantities

Greens (collard, mustard, beet, carrot)	Leaf lettuces (dark types)	Grated root crops, such as carrots and beets
Dandelions	Romaine lettuce	Green cabbage leaves
Nasturtium	Alfalfa pellets	Peas and other legumes
Broccoli leaves (not the stems or florets)	Mulberry leaves and berries	Okra
Hibiscus blooms and leaves	Grated squashes	Green onions
Escarole	Bok Choy	Yellow beans
	Rose petals	

Limited Quantities

Apple	Melons	Tofu
Avocado	Papaya	Tomato
Berries (straw, blue, elder, etc.)	Plums	Peaches
	Pear	

Are my sprouts ready to eat yet? You can grow some of your own iguana food (we tried sprouting parrot mix here), but your iguana's appetite will require much more than this small appetizer.

per.) Check with your veterinarian to see if a dietary stimulant might be in order. Continue to provide water for your iguana in the normal fashion during this changeover; you want it to be hungry, not dehydrated.

Commercial Diets

Many types of commercially prepared "complete" iguana diets are now available.

Since these are generally dried foods, they can offer no moisture to your iguana. If used as a sole food source, they can contribute to dehydration and constipation, especially in egg-carrying females.

We use commercial diets as an augmentation to our iguanas' regular diet, and they seem to enjoy the change; at least when we offer these foods, they are readily eaten. Having a container of iguana-acceptable

iguana food on the shelf and readily accessible may mean you don't have to go shopping at midnight when it's snowing. Just be sure to either add water or have fresh water available.

Water: Having clean fresh water readily available for both drinking and bathing is of extreme importance to your iguana. Some keepers provide a smaller dish for drinking. Since iguanas often defecate in standing water, their receptacle should be cleaned and refilled daily.

The Iguana Dietary Machine

How do all these dietary admonitions work regarding the iguana? Why does it make a difference when you chop foods, and why do some hatchlings grow much more slowly than others? Researchers have made major contributions to our knowledge about the remarkable workings of the iguana's dietary system.

Coprophagy and Digestion

Digesting plant cellulose requires a complex gut and a great number of microflora. The significance of bacteria and protozoans to digestion in other herbivorous organisms— higher vertebrates and insects—is already understood; termites, for instance, cannot digest cellulose without their gut protozoans. For iguanas, the microflora bacteria actually ferment the food items in the gut, releasing the food value to the iguana, and the helminths once thought to be parasitic may aid digestion by churning the food in the gut. But the iguanas aren't born with microflora. It's acquired through coprophagy—the eating of feces.

Hatchlings that are captive hatched and captive raised will grow more slowly than hatchlings in the wild. They don't have a chance to develop the hindgut flora present in hatchlings from the wild, and as a result, cannot digest their food as efficiently. (Captive iguanas that are given antibiotics as part of a medical regimen may need reinoculation to reestablish their gut flora.) Two of these indicator hindgut microflora are a bacterial complex, *Lampropedia merismopediodes*, and a large ciliate protozoan, probably a holotrich like those found in rumen of cattle and sheep.

Katherine Troyer investigated how the gut bacteria/protozoan ciliate are transferred to the hatchlings. She used the ciliate as the marker organism, because it's more delicate than the bacteria. If the ciliate survives a transfer, the bacteria would certainly survive. She found that hatchlings don't acquire the gut flora as they hatch from the egg and crawl through the soil to first look at the world. Captive hatchlings housed with a one-month-old wild hatchling all developed the ciliate, indicating transference among hatchlings. Captive-bred hatchlings fed adult fecal material for ten days developed the protozoan, and these iguanas grew faster than the control group; they also assimilated their food significantly better than the control group.

Indirect contact with the adults seemed to be the key. In the wild, hatchling iguanas preferentially position themselves in the tree canopy near the adults for the first three weeks of their lives. Although no young hatchlings were seen to eat adult feces during this time, three that were sacrificed and examined had fecal matter in their stomachs. During the next four to six weeks of their lives, the baby iguanas move lower in the vegetation, and they are positioned at random, away from the adults.

The Hindgut

Even with abundant gut microflora, plant material is difficult to digest. The microflora in the iguana's gut are activated at a temperature of 85°F (29°C) or above. An iguana kept at a temperature below this simply cannot digest its food. It must bask to raise its body temperature.

There may be more than just bacteria and protozoans at work. John Iverson found that the iguanid hindgut routinely harbors enormous populations of nematodes. His estimate of more than 15,000 nematodes in the colon of a healthy adult *Cyclura carinata* indicates the quantity under discussion. Iverson suggests it is probable that colon partitions provide important microhabitats for colic symbionts, and that nematodes, like protozoans and bacteria, are among these symbionts.

This isn't a case of just one kind of nematode really doing well in the colon of iguanids. Multiple species are involved, and it seems that the number of species that can be harbored is directly related to the number of valves in the hindgut. For the green iguana, with its seven valves, eight species of nematodes are not uncommon, but the number of nematode species is also tied to the size of the iguana. The green iguana evidently accumulates the species over time, because it isn't until the iguana's snout-vent length is almost 13 inches (32 cm) that the species number reaches eight. What good those numbers and species of nematodes can possibly do is still unknown. Perhaps the nematodes, through the mechanical action of crawling through the gut contents, help mix and break down the food, increasing the surface area for digestion; maybe they produce waste products such as vitamins, cellulase (an enzyme that breaks down cellulose) or fatty acids that themselves are used by the iguanas.

Fatty acids: Volatile fatty acids (VFAs) are the product of the bacterial fermentation process, and these are assimilated by the green iguana. Research by Richard McBee and Virginia McBee has revealed that anywhere from 30 to 40 percent of the iguana's energy requirements are produced by the fermentation activity in the gut. The McBees feel the efficiency of hindgut fermentation—predigestion in effect, done by a second party—is that the iguana can spend less time eating, and less time exposed to predators. We suggest that the advantage is that the iguana may spend less time eating, and more time displaying/seeking a mate. Hindgut fermentation also allows the iguana to eat and survive on types and amounts of vegetation it could not otherwise assimilate.

Iguana Snacks

Iguanas do snack on high-energy foods such as insects when the opportunity arises. I (RDB) have sat in iguana habitats in several Latin American countries and watched wild baby iguanas animatedly chase down and eat many species of insects. They seem to especially favor various orthopterans such as grasshoppers and crickets. I have seen the same behavior exhibited by feral iguanas in Dade County, Florida.

or whether this occurs only in the hatchling to juvenile sizes. Is insect consumption an effort to compensate for their smaller size/less efficient digestive systems? We suspect that insect consumption continues opportunistically throughout life, but may decrease as the agility of the iguana decreases with size.

What none of us now deny is that captive green iguanas fed even moderate amounts of animal protein often develop gout and bone problems. But again, there have been few studies done on whether captive iguanas kept in outside facilities and given opportunities to exercise are less prone to these problems than green iguanas kept indoors. Certainly a large cage in which your iguana can exercise and full-spectrum lighting—or better yet, natural unfiltered sunlight—will help offset dietary mistakes you might make.

What is not yet known is whether these wild and feral iguanas continue to eat insects throughout their lives,

Factors That Affect the Efficiency of Hindgut Fermentation

• The iguana must be warm enough, with a body temperature between 80 and 94°F (27–36°C).
• The moisture content of the food; this drops to 23 to 30 percent during the dry season.
• The consumption of fruit, with its higher levels of fermentable carbohydrates than leaves.

• The variety and state of the leaves consumed; leaves during the dry season are tougher and drier than during the rainy season.
• The rate at which the fermentation acids are absorbed. Unabsorbed volatile fatty acids mean a lower pH in the gut, which means a slower fermentation rate.

Chapter Nine

Health Notes

Metabolic Bone Disease

Metabolic bone disease (MBD) is one of the most prevalent and insidious health disorders associated with captive great green iguanas and other herbivorous and omnivorous lizards. MBD is a potentially fatal, crippling, nutritional disorder that is entirely preventable. Once present, however, it is less easily corrected, and physical imperfections are seldom reversible.

In simplified terms, MBD is the removal of needed calcium from the bones. This leaching occurs when, due to a lousy diet, your iguana's blood calcium level has dropped too low.

In nature, it is light waves in the ultraviolet range (specifically UVB) that allow vitamin D_3 to be formed. The D_3, in turn, permits calcium uptake.

To prevent MBD, the husbandry of your iguana must provide the full-spectrum lighting so your iguana can make its own D_3, or you must add D_3 to the diet. The food offered to your iguana *must* be primarily high-quality, calcium-rich, leafy greens and/or a specifically developed and veterinary-approved iguana diet that contains at least two times more calcium than phosphorus.

MBD has been called many other things. Among these are swollen leg disease, rubber-jaw, bone decalcification, and rickets. All of these terms describe at least one sad manifestation of the disease. External manifestations include a softened jawbone and skull, swollen limbs, fragile bones, impaired mobility, difficulty eating (due to a "rubber" mouth), and a resulting loss of weight, and limb spasms, tics, and/or twitches.

If any of these symptoms appear, check and update your iguana's diet and seek veterinary help immediately. When MBD is present, a radiograph can easily identify suboptimal bone density. Other tests can determine blood calcium levels. Tests and medications can be very expensive. It is mandatory that you then follow the remedial instructions of your veterinarian regarding lighting, dietary supplements, and diet-content—to the letter. Remember that with proper diet and lighting MBD need never occur.

The Skin

Iguanas have a relatively tough keratinized skin that serves as a literal barrier between them and the outside world of pathogens. Problems can arise when the skin is torn or damaged, particularly when the animal has been stressed by crowding, shipping, and poor environmental conditions such as a dirty cage or lack of sufficient clean water and food. Diseases, particularly those of the skin, can be infectious or noninfectious, although one sort of problem generally leads to another. Once a problem with the skin has been eliminated, the iguana generally sheds off the damaged areas within a few sheds.

Shedding

Skin shedding is a normal process that takes place three or four times a year. The peeling generally begins along the face and the backbone, and the unpigmented outer layer of skin is shed in patches. The whole process takes a day or so to complete. Shedding is a no-worry sort of process; it is entirely normal and simply facilitates growth. All you need to do is make sure the cage is humid enough so the skin will slough off easily; if the skin sticks and can't be sloughed off, increase the humidity by misting the iguana twice daily—remember to aim the spray so the mist falls like rain—or by swimming your iguana in warm water just deep enough to cover its back. A five-minute swim daily for three days should do it. Do examine your iguana to make sure that no constricting bands of skin are left on the toes, and as irresistible as helping your iguana may seem, allow it to shed on its own; you don't need to help peel the loose patches off.

Abscesses

Abscesses are essentially "walled-off" infections. Bacteria, fungus, or a parasite enters the body—through trauma such as a sharp stick or branch that hits at the right angle and enters the skin; a larger iguana bites a smaller iguana, and tears the skin; the iguana is kept in a crowded, wet cage and is scratched by another iguana's toenails—and reproduces. The body responds by isolating that infection, resulting in a hard, round, raised/swollen area called an abscess.

The face of a healthy iguana. The early signs of MBD can be seen in an iguana's face. Look critically for foreshortened nose, an undershot jaw, or eyes that seem to bulge a bit from a small (weakened) skull.

Although it may look awkward, the skin pieces fall off of their own accord.

In the wild, where an iguana can bask to raise its body temperature even higher than normal basking temperatures, eat a normal diet, or select special foods, and avoid stress, with time the iguana's immune system can usually literally overcome the pathogen.

In captivity, where the iguana may be less able to determine its body temperature or select its diet, time tends to work against the body's effort to deal with an abscess. That's where you, or rather your reptile veterinarian, comes in.

Your reptile veterinarian will open the abscess, drain it, and diagnose the cause. He or she will prescribe a fungicide, parasiticide, or antibiotics to deal with the infection.

Viral Diseases

Abscesses are not the only problem that affect an iguana's skin; viral diseases are another.

Papillomatosis: The best known viral disease is papillomatosis, which is found in one form or another in European green lizards and in sea turtles. There is no treatment, except for surgical excision, and the tumors may reappear. Thirty years ago, papillomatosis was a rarity in captive collections and in sea turtles, and none has been reported in iguanas to date. Iguanas do not normally

Your Own Health and Salmonella

Salmonella is a bacteria that is found almost everywhere. Most of us know about salmonella from reading about chicken salad at picnics, or children with pet turtles. Concerns about salmonella and young children resulted in laws forbidding the sale of any turtles with less than a 3-inch (7.6 cm) shell length.

Salmonella becomes a problem to humans when we ingest or take in this bacterium. Typical symptoms are nausea, vomiting, diarrhea, cramps, loss of appetite, and low-grade fever, all typical symptoms of what most people would call food poisoning, or what happens when you somehow acquire this bacterium.

One way is to allow your iguana access to food preparation areas. Another would be to kiss your iguana. You don't really have to kiss the iguana to pick up salmonella from it; you just have to touch it or touch something it has touched, and then touch your lips. Young children are especially known for putting anything they can pick up in their mouths—who hasn't seen a baby gravely gnawing on a set of car keys? Babies don't even have to have personal contact with a reptile that carries salmonella. Babies only have to touch where the reptile has crawled, or stooled, and then put their fingers in their mouths. Babies and very young children do not have fully developed immune systems, and salmonella can be very serious or even fatal. Salmonella is also very serious for someone with a suppressed or compromised immune system.

It's simple to see how easy it is to contract salmonella. It also easy to see that simply washing your hands after you handle/feed/pet/clean/move your iguana will help avoid the problem. Keeping your iguana's cage very clean, including washing the dishes in soapy water and dipping them in a dilute (5 percent) chlorine bleach solution and rinsing, will also help prevent the spread of many types of bacteria. If you let your iguana swim in your bathtub—and we don't really recommend this—clean the tub with the dilute bleach solution as soon as you take the iguana out.

come into contact with lizards from Europe, but the increased market for pet reptiles from around the world and humans' inherent desire to provide "company" for their pets, may change this. (Remember, unless you're absolutely certain about the health of your reptiles, community caging has very real risks.)

Dermatophytosis: This is an opportunistic fungal infection of the skin (derma, skin; phyta, fungus; tosis, infection). It is generally seen in newly imported young and hatchling iguanas. (Credit for the development of treatment techniques is due Margaret Wissman, DVM, DABVP.)

Fungal Infections

Young iguanas are kept in large holding pens in the iguana farms in Central and South America. Depending on the facility, the pens may be suspended above the ground, or they may sit directly on the ground. Small ponds or large water containers in the pens allow the iguanas to soak, and during the days, the pens may be sprayed with water to help keep the iguanas cool. During the rainy season in Central and South America (our wintertime), moisture can build up in the cages. The crowded conditions under which most of the hatchlings are kept result in the iguanas stacking on top of each other during the day to sun and sleep, and crawl across each other; even if there are only two iguanas in an enclosure, you'll find them sleeping, sunning, and crawling over each other. But crowded conditions can result in bites and scratches. When the skin is broken, any pathogen present in the air, the soil, the water, or on the skin of another iguana can move right in. And that's exactly what happens.

New imports that arrive in the U.S. from October to March may display some black, crusty lesions that may look superficially like a minor problem. Skin scrapings may reveal severe inflammation—a fungus—within the skin layers themselves. A fungus, *Geotrichum candidum*, has been identified along with two bacteria, *Pseudomonas* sp. and *Aeromonas* sp.

If the animal is kept warm, with time, the offending lesions are generally sloughed off and the animal survives, but this is a contagious problem, so separation of the affected lizard from all other animals is important. If the animal has been stressed or kept in substandard conditions, it may not be strong enough to deal with the fungal infection.

Treatment: Veterinary care for an animal with these lesions includes good husbandry and antifungal medication. Start with good food, warmth, light, a dry environment, and deworming, if necessary, to create a healthful environment, both inside and outside the iguana. Soak the affected skin areas with a dilute povidone-iodine solution; Betadyne

Going for a swim. Dehydrated iguanas benefit from a swim in a bathtub. Keep the water at about 90 degrees and disinfect the tub afterward.

The rasp-like skin is the primary barricade against infection. The exterior layer, the cuticle, is shed in large pieces at regular intervals.

would serve the same function. Be certain your iguana doesn't ingest any of the solution.

The iguana's appetite may be depressed during this illness. Depending on the severity and duration of the fungal infection, you may need to tube-feed your iguana until its appetite returns. Baby-food pureed peas and green beans are two food choices, delivered through a 1-cc syringe case, past the iguana's tongue. You could also use a supplement called Emeraid II.

Because the fungus lives in the upper layers of skin, this simple treatment may be all that's needed. The area of the lesion should be reduced in size, and look paler than it did before treatment. Several sheds may be needed before all signs of the fungal infection disappear.

The causative agent, *Geotrichum candidum*, is not entirely a benign agent. It has been involved in human mold infections affecting the lungs, skin, digestive tract, eyes, and wound infections. Although no trans-

mission from iguana to human has been reported, it is important to wash your hands before and after working with your infected iguana. If your immune system is compromised, let someone else house, feed, and treat your iguana.

Respiratory Ailments

Respiratory ailments in baby iguanas—especially stressed baby iguanas—can be a very real, and potentially fatal, problem.

Shipping Temperatures

Respiratory ailments can be brought on in many ways, not the least important being shipping temperatures. Despite the fact that most airplanes have temperature-moderated and fully pressurized belly bins in which live animals are shipped, potential for encountering temperature fluctuations exists in all but the very best of weather.

Chilling may occur if, while an aircraft is flying at a high altitude, as virtually all now do, bin ventilation is impaired due to improper or excessive loading. Chilling may also occur during cold weather, when an airplane makes an intermediate stop and bin doors are opened and left open for an hour or more for the purpose of loading and unloading, or perhaps at a transfer point where a live shipment is allowed to remain on a chilled ramp for an excessive period of time—and in very cold

Isolating the New Iguana

If you already have an iguana, and bring another into your house, no matter what the source is, keep the two iguanas separate for at least three weeks while you watch the new iguana to make certain it isn't bringing some type of pathogen into your home.

• Set up a separate cage in a different room, and practice good hygiene.

• Wash your hands before you handle, feed or clean either iguana, and afterward as well.

• Keep their food and water dishes separate until you've cleaned them thoroughly.

• Have a stool specimen from the new iguana tested—you might as well have your "regular" iguana's stool tested at the same time—for worms or other pathogens.

• Watch the new iguana for signs of listlessness, chubby limbs that may portend MBD (metabolic bone disease), and lack of appetite, and treat any illness that appears.

• At the end of the isolation period, if your caging is large enough and if the iguanas are of different sexes or both females, you can put them together, and be essentially certain that you aren't spreading a disease from one to the other. If both of your iguanas are males, you can't cage them together and you may not be able to place their cages in the same room (see Chapter Four, Behavior).

temperatures, "excessive" can be a surprisingly short duration.

Improper husbandry, such as nights with too low temperatures, cages with cold drafts, or the buildup of an untenable parasite load, or accidents, such as losing heating or electricity during a winter storm, can also cause respiratory distress. If quickly warmed and properly cared for after only a few hours of adverse conditions, baby iguanas may be little worse for the wear. But if the problems begin by adverse shipping conditions or other accidental chillings are compounded by anything less than ideal husbandry immediately following such an ordeal, severe respiratory distress may occur.

Reptiles are slow to show the ultimate effects of improper handling. The baby iguanas may arrive at their destination and be running agilely about, even feeding well, for several days before the respiratory problem manifests itself. Then, one morning, you turn on the cage lights and feed the little creature, only to find that instead of looking alertly at you and ravenously attacking its food, the lizard is listless, has closed eyes, and a runny nose. And while we all know that prevention is the ideal policy, what is your recourse if this unpleasant scenario occurs?

Signs: Besides lethargic demeanor and a runny nose, respiratory ailments are often accompanied by sneezing and unnaturally rapid, often shallow, breathing. As the respiratory ailment worsens, rasping and bubbling may accompany each of your iguana's breaths. At this stage the respiratory distress is critical and often fatal.

Treatment of Respiratory Infections

If, despite all of your efforts, a respiratory infection occurs, elevate the cage's basking area to a temperature of 96 to 98°F (35.6–37°C)—keep the cool end at 88 to 92°F (31–33.3°C)—then immediately call your reptile-oriented veterinarian for suggestions. If the elevated temperatures do not cause symptoms of respiratory distress to lessen within a day or two, antibiotic treatment will be necessary.

There are many "safe" drugs available, but some respiratory ailments do not respond well to these. The newer aminoglycoside drugs are more effective, but correspondingly more dangerous. There is little latitude in dosage amounts and the iguana must be well hydrated to ensure against renal (kidney) damage. It is thought that the injection site for aminoglycosides must be anterior to mid-body to assure that the renal-portal system is not compromised. It is mandatory that your veterinarian be well acquainted with reptilian medicine to be sure the correct decisions are made.

Preventing Respiratory Ailments

Here are some suggestions to help you prevent the occurrence of a respiratory ailment:
• Keep your iguana happy and healthy; prevent stress!
• Cage your iguana properly; prevent chilling and drafts.
• If kept with one or more cagemates, be sure all are compatible.

Mechanical Injuries

Like slamming your finger in a car door, iguanas sometimes suffer mechanical injuries from being in the wrong place at the wrong time. These injuries, while they don't start with an infectious agent, can become infected if no precautions are taken. Listed here are some of the more common mechanical injuries of iguanas. Iguanas, like small children, can find an amazing number of ways to get into trouble, or to become injured. Larger ones that may be allowed to roam your home while you're there need to be restricted to a large cage, or a bathroom, when no one is at home.

Burns

One of the saddest of mechanical injuries is a burn, because a burn is usually avoidable and burns take a long time to heal. Burns occur when your iguana has a chance to warm itself too close to an incandescent light bulb, or if the lizard rests/sleeps on a heated branch or rock and the device's thermostat is too high or malfunctioning. Iguanas are not the smartest creatures, and evolution has not prepared them in any way for captivity. In the wild, sunlight may make them hot, but they can move away from sunlight, and it never gets hot enough to lead to burns. Branches and rocks heat up slowly in the sun, giving an iguana time to become aware of a potential problem. Iguanas are very slow to react to a too-hot surface. They'll snuggle right up to an unshielded light bulb, or stay on a hot rock or branch until you smell something cooking—and it's the iguana!

Shield your light bulb; a simple cage of half-inch (13 mm) hardware cloth bent around the bulb will work. The iguana should not be able to get any closer than 4 inches (10 cm) from the bulb. If you must use hot rocks and hot branches during the winter months, check them weekly to make certain they are functioning correctly.

Part of the problem with hot rocks and heated branches is that iguanas are heliothermic. Their response to too much heat from below is not as acute as the sense that tells them it's time to get out of the sun. Because we feel hot rocks and hot branches are an unnatural way to heat an iguana, and because they are so difficult and time consuming to monitor, we don't use them.

Treatment: How can you tell if your iguana is burned? Burns rarely blister, and may appear as discolored areas. Depending on the damage to the layers of skin, the area may ooze serum. Minor burns need to be kept clean and dry. An antibiotic cream might be needed, because the integrity of the skin has been altered and opportunistic bacteria like *Pseudomonas* can move right in. Keep an eye on your iguana's appetite after a burn; if the food intake lessens or stops, or if the burns are severe, take your iguana to the veterinarian.

Nose Injuries

Iguanas may rub their noses against the mesh of the bag they are shipped in. They may run into the side of the cages in an effort to escape, or to get away from you or from another iguana. It doesn't matter much if the cage surface is smooth or rough; enough rubbing will abrade any nose. This behavior is especially true for larger iguanas that are wild-caught. They frighten more easily than smaller iguanas, and they are strong enough to really damage their noses when they run into a nonyielding surface.

Nose injuries are not uncommon, and in themselves, are not life-threatening. If you can remove the reason or the agent for the rubbing early in the process, the nose will heal on its own. It's when the injury is combined with a pathogen, or when the health of the iguana has been compromised through poor diet (see the section on MBD, page 107) that you run into serious problems.

Treatment: Give the iguana as large a cage as you can, to increase its feeling of freedom. You can cover three sides of the cage on the outside with an opaque surface so the iguana will not try to run "through" the sides. Paper or lightweight fabric works well; both let light through but obstruct the iguana's vision. The reason you cover three sides and not all four is to help your iguana get used to you. If you covered all four sides, every time the iguana saw you, it would react as if it saw you for the first time. By covering three sides of the cage on the outside, and suspending a soft cloth inside the cage, just halfway up the side of the cage and 2 inches (5.1 cm) away from the fourth side, your iguana can see you and can run, but will still encounter that soft cloth surface.

Toe Injuries

Broken limbs or toes: Iguanas can get their toes and claws caught in the mesh of a cage top or side, or

they can catch their toes in the cage furniture, become startled, move suddenly, and injure themselves that way. Sometimes the limb or toe is caught in the bag used to transport the iguanas from the wholesalers. Subadult to adult iguanas captured in the wild may have their back legs twisted up over their backs and tied together to prevent them from escaping. In captivity, metabolic bone disease (MBD) can cause the toes and all bones to become fragile and rubbery, but if this is the case, the broken toe is the least of your iguana's worries; see the section on MBD, page 107.

Whatever the reason, a broken limb or toe needs to be immobilized—splinted, if possible—until it heals. Your veterinarian may recommend taping a splinted hind limb to the iguana's tail. For a broken toe, a short length of aquarium tubing, if it's large enough to slip over the toe, can be adhesive-taped in place for a couple of weeks or until the toe heals. If it's a wild-caught adult or if the aquarium tubing isn't possible, see if you can adhesive-tape the toe to its neighbor, and immobilize it that way. Be certain during the healing period of two to four weeks that the diet includes a calcium supplement, and avoid panicking your iguana with sudden moves around its cage.

Sometimes you get an iguana with an old toe break that hasn't healed and the toe has died and

You can use a pair of nail clippers to trim the tips of an iguana's too-long nails.

Trauma from Falls

Although great green iguanas may be high-dive champions in the wild, cascading precipitously when startled from well-elevated perches into water or, occasionally, onto yielding leaf litter under their tree, even a short drop onto a nonyielding surface by a captive may result in serious injury to the lizard.

In a drop of less than 4 feet (1.2 m), let's say from the top of a kitchen shelf to the floor below, a large iguana may break leg bones or more seriously, its backbone. In many cases, if the lizard is in good condition, with bones of proper density, a leg break can be splinted and will heal. Spinal injuries, however, often cause permanently reduced mobility or even total rear-quarter paralysis.

Although falls can occur in cages, they seem to be more often the result of a free-roaming or sleeping iguana being startled, or making a misstep. Can this danger be completely alleviated?

Probably not. But by providing secure perches with ample clawholds for your iguana, and by taking reasonable care not to startle the lizard while it is napping complacently, or exploring an elevated area that does not provide good footholds, the possibility of a fall can be reduced.

It is also imperative that your iguana's bone density be optimal. If the lizard's bones are weakened by improper diet, breaks may occur during normal climbing and other such routine activities.

Again, we emphasize the importance of safe quarters, proper diet, and of knowing the whereabouts of a reptile-oriented veterinarian, just in case his or her services are needed.

turned black, or infection has set in. In cases like this, amputation of the toe may be the right decision, but this decision should be made with the help of your veterinarian.

Broken toenails: Toenails get broken for the same reason as toes, and perhaps even more frequently when the iguana is removed from a screen or mesh side of its cage too quickly to allow it to disengage its toes. Use a styptic pencil to staunch any bleeding. If you don't have anything else, a few cotton fibers from a cotton ball, wrapped around the bleeding portion of the nail, will help provide enough surface area and air exposure to promote clotting. This kind of injury generally heals without any problems or infection if you keep the foot clean and dry for a few days, but should problems develop, talk to your veterinarian.

Trimming nails: The giant green iguana is a climber. To help with this habit, their claws are sharp and recurved. In the wild, normal activity levels keep the nail worn down. In captivity, few iguanas have the opportunity to run and climb extensively. At the same time, those long nails are efficient tools in discouraging handling. You may need to trim the tip end of your iguana's nails. To do so:

• Simply immobilize your iguana; wrapping/rolling it securely in a large towel helps—leave the head and one foot exposed.

• Use a pair of human nail clippers or a pair of animal nail clippers to gently nip off the curved end of the nail.

• Avoid clipping into the blood vessel in the nail; if you do nick it, use a styptic pencil or cotton fibers (see page 117) to staunch the bleeding.

Toes and shed skin: Occasionally, the iguana will not shed all of its skin, especially if the cage humidity is too low. A ringlet of dried skin may remain on one or more toes. Moisten the dried skin with warm water or a bit of baby oil, give it a moment to soften, and gently take it off. Left in place, these dried skin ringlets tend to act as constriction bands on the iguana's toes, cutting off the blood supply to the toe. If this happens, there is rarely any swelling or obvious signs of a problem. The distal portion of the toe simply blackens as the tissue dies. Then the dead portion of the toe dries out and drops off, a preventable event for the alert owner if this problem is caught in time.

Broken Tail

Wild-caught iguanas may come in with broken tails, and the causes are varied. Generally, the pursuer is almost close enough to grab the iguana but grabs the tail instead.

Bleeding from a broken tail is minimal for young iguanas, and the regeneration process begins. The regrown tail is shorter than the missing section, stiffer, and colored more dully than the original, but none of these conditions presents a problem to the iguana. The important thing to remember is that the broken portion needs to be removed completely, and that a clean, complete break heals quicker than a partial break where the tissues may be torn.

When a tail break occurs in the last half of the tail, regeneration is generally almost complete. When the break occurs near the body, the wound may need a clotting agent to lessen the blood loss.

Endoparasites

Endoparasites are not a big problem for most iguanas, even if these parasites are present. The relationship, as odd as this term may seem, between an iguana and its endoparasites is generally a stalemate only as long as the parasites don't gain the upper hand and kill the iguana. The nematode burden that iguanas from some areas in the wild bear indicates there may be some form of a symbiotic relationship.

Symptoms

It's when the iguana is weakened by some other problem—poor diet,

improper housing, or illness such as MBD or a respiratory illness—that the drain on the iguana by endoparasites can become lethal. Symptoms of a heavy endoparasitic load include lethargy and poor feeding response, which can seem pretty nebulous. It's the combination of clues—a new iguana, recently stressed, perhaps straight from the wild, looks relatively healthy, but its responses seem a little slow, it won't eat and seems to rest a lot, even for an iguana—that tells you that you need to take your iguana to the veterinarian. The reason you need the veterinarian's knowledge and skills is to identify the problem and develop the treatment plan. The symptoms of internal parasites may match the symptoms of a respiratory ailment, so proper diagnosis is important.

Diagnosis

Your veterinarian can diagnose some endoparasites by a stool sample and others by a small blood sample. The most common intestinal parasites are roundworms and tapeworms, both internal helminths, and they generally occupy the intestine. Other internal parasites include flukes, which favor the liver and gallbladder, the pentasomids, which stay in the lungs, and filariid worms. Filarids may stay in body organs or wander about the body cavity; their offspring migrate to the bloodstream. There they may be taken up by a blood-sucking insect such as the mosquito, and transported to another iguana.

Treatment

The medications your veterinarian uses will depend on which type of intestinal parasite your iguana may have, but the medications used are pretty much the same as those used against internal parasites in other animals.

Ectoparasites

Ticks

Ectoparasites are those easy-to-see ticks found on iguanas and the not-as-easily seen mites. Both are eight-legged spider relatives that are blood drinkers. Of the two, the ticks are more common, and it's easier to get rid of them. Use one of the commercial tick removers that works like a pair of plunger-powered tweezers to remove ticks.

Mites

Mites are much smaller; until you know what to look for, they are hard to see. The good news is that mite infestations on green iguanas are rare. If you think that mites could be present, look for black or red dots about the size of the period at the end of this sentence. Mites tend to gather in skin pockets, such as around the iguana's eyes or in its armpits. Their feces tend to impart a silvery sheen to the lizard's skin, but unless you know what you're looking at, you might not recognize what the sheen means. Because of their small size, and the even smaller size of their eggs, mites are very readily spread throughout a reptile collection, or transferred from one cage to another by a careless hobbyist. If you handle someone else's iguana, or if you take care of someone else's iguana while he or she is on vacation, wash your hands before you handle your own iguana.

Treatment: If your iguana does become infested with mites, there are several ways to get rid of them. Your veterinarian can prescribe an oral or spray-on treatment. An insecticidal spray safe enough for puppies and kittens can be sprayed on a cloth, and the iguana wiped down with the cloth; don't spray the iguana directly. You can purchase mite treatment sprays at your pet store or online.

Chapter Ten

Breeding

In the United States, herpetoculture seems more fueled by profit than by altruism. Although great green iguanas will breed rather readily in captivity, while imported specimens continue to be available for the current low prices, there is little incentive for hobbyists to set up breeding colonies.

Protecting Great Green Iguanas

Panama and Nicaragua have banned the hunting of the green iguana and its eggs, which are especially valued for their alleged aphrodisiac qualities. The ban is especially aimed toward protecting the females during the egg-laying season. The egg hunters catch the females, remove her eggs, and sew up the incision. The female is released, but since the ovaries are removed along with the eggs, she is unable to breed again, if she survives the crude surgery. Critics of the ban point out that the poorer natives are the ones who will be punished by the law, since they are the ones with limited choices in their supply of protein. To

help replace the decreased numbers of iguanas in the wild, small-scale farming of the green iguana has begun. One source of funding is the Shinmatsu Foundation. The Foundation distributed baby iguanas to poor families, the idea being that the iguanas will be raised much like chickens for their flesh and their eggs. The National Association for the Conservation of Nature is raising baby iguanas on a farm north of Panama City, the capital of Panama, for release into the nearby forests.

Great green iguanas are also the subject of large-scale pet-farming operations in several of the Latin American countries where they occur. From dozens to hundreds of breeder iguanas are housed and allowed to breed in outdoor pens. Given the fact that the clutch of an average-sized adult female iguana often numbers more than 25 eggs (occasionally more than 70!), the number of babies produced from only a few successfully incubated clutches can be quite considerable.

Hatchlings produced at these farming operations are being used both in rerelease programs attempting to enhance dwindling wild populations, and as a cash crop for the pet trade. Iguana pet farming has resulted in hatchling iguanas being readily and inexpensively available to the pet market during much of the year and is reducing the numbers of babies taken from the wild.

Unfortunately, neither program deals with the loss of habitat for the iguanas, and all the other creatures that live in the forests with them. Panama, for example, has lost 40 percent of its natural forest since the 1940s.

Except for programs involving very desirable and expensive morphs such as albinos, when hobbyists do breed iguanas, it is usually in very small numbers. This may be as much a question of the quite considerable cage space required as of the low monetary yield. Should you be interested in trying your luck, we offer a few suggestions here.

Cycling

Naturally occurring seasonal climatic changes such as photoperiod, temperature, rainfall, and relative humidity influence the life cycle of the iguana. Even captive iguanas are sensitive to at least some of these changes. Should you choose to increase your chances for breeding success, you should enhance as many of these natural phenomena as possible, either naturally or artificially, for your iguanas. If you are among the growing number of iguana owners who live in the Sun-belt, especially in southern Florida and the Lower Rio Grande Valley of Texas, you may need to do nothing more than to house your iguanas in spacious outdoor cages. It is quite likely that Mother Nature will take care of the photoperiod.

Photoperiod

The term *photoperiod* simply refers to the hours of daylight, as opposed to the hours of darkness, in any given day. Photoperiod is more seasonally variable at or near the Poles than at the Equator. The hours of daylight increase as winter gives way to spring and spring to summer, then decrease again in the fall.

We suggest that a natural photoperiod is best. Check the weather page in your local newspaper for the exact sunrise and sunset times, and periodically (about weekly) alter the number of hours that your cage is artificially illuminated to coincide with the naturally occurring photoperiod. In many cases, if your iguanas are housed next to a window, the natural photoperiod may actually outshine artificial illumination. If your lizard is housed outside, no supplemental lighting will be needed. Iguanas are diurnal, heliotropic, heliothermic lizards. That is:

1. They are active by day.

2. They are drawn to sunlit areas.

3. They thermoregulate by availing themselves of sun-provided warmth.

These are three of the criteria that you should try hard to provide and duplicate. A fourth is increased cage

Intruder beware. Simon Garfunkle, in full breeding readiness, pauses during feeding to display to an intruder. Note jowl distension.

humidity—frequent misting, partially covering the cage, and/or a larger water receptacle will accomplish this—during the very warm days of spring, summer, and early fall.

If you do not have sunny, warm, outdoor facilities for your iguana, very brilliant (preferably UVA- and UVB-producing) artificial light and suitable warmth must be provided. Do remember, though, that warmth without light is not satisfactory for iguanas, or for any other heliothermic lizard. Generally speaking, you should provide the lowest humidity, the fewest hours of daylight, and the lowest temperatures (but by only a few degrees) in midwinter.

Altering Temperatures

Temperatures, both daily and seasonal, can be altered with the prudent use of lights and/or heating elements. Iguanas are subjected in the wild to one or two rapid drops of several degrees daily brought about by rainstorms. It is not necessary, but it may help, to duplicate these mini-fluctuations of temperature to facilitate breeding. There is a winter drop in relative humidity, likely in captivity as well, and also during that season, a several degree drop of nighttime from daytime temperature. If you are trying to elevate nighttime temperatures, use a red or a blue bulb. It seems that the light from either is less intrusive than from a white bulb and your iguanas will sleep normally.

Conditioning and Feeding

To produce healthy eggs that develop into robust hatchlings, your breeder iguanas must themselves be in good condition. They should have good body weight, be free of excessive burdens of endoparasites, have had ample full-spectrum lighting, and be fully hydrated. *Do not breed them otherwise.*

Your lizards should be fed heavily throughout the year. Because a female's appetite will wane for two to four weeks prior to egg deposition, it is particularly important that your iguanas enter the breeding period in top condition. Be sure to provide sufficient calcium and D_3 throughout the year. These additives are especially important when the females are laying down eggshells. If your female becomes dehydrated while she is carrying eggs, it may be difficult for her to lay.

Courtship and Reproduction

Both wild and captive male iguanas herald reproductive readiness with brightened body color, more frequent and more strenuous territorial and courtship displays, and less tolerance for normal overtures by other iguanas, by family pets, or by their keeper. A female that is old enough to breed tends to increase her food intake dramatically just before breeding season begins.

Colors: An iguana's breeding colors vary, seemingly by geographical origin, from a brilliant green to any one of several shades of orange, both colors either with or without black barring or areas of dusky pigment.

Displays: Courtship and territorial displays involve rapid distending and furling of the dewlap, head bobs, a vertical flattening of the body, full extension of the forelimbs, and anterior pushups. When this behavior is noted, be very careful when approaching a dominant male.

A receptive female iguana may approach or ignore a displaying male, but if she is near enough for the male to see her, and emitting pheromones, the male will grasp, and attempt to breed her anyway. Unless she acquiesces, the attempt is very likely to fail, but the female can be injured during the attempt. If successful, copulation lasts from a few minutes to about a quarter of an hour.

When and How Do Iguanas Breed?

The great green iguana is an oviparous lizard. Wild females in a given population ovulate at pretty much the same time every year. In Panama, female iguanas ovulate at about the same time, breed from December to January (the dry months), then journey to an island to dig burrows for their eggs.

In captivity, all bets are off. Some pairs have bred in October, some in June, and others in all months between. It is possible that we soon will have records for captive iguanas breeding during all months of the year.

Prior to copulation, a male iguana will restrain a female by grasping the side of her neck or her nape in his jaws. During these interactions the neck of a female iguana may become moderately to seriously abraded. Males will attempt to breed so persistently that it may be necessary to separate the pair to prevent serious injury to the female. It is best if there is not a significant difference in size between the two.

Thwarting Iguana Aggression

We must start this section by reminding you that although an iguana may be tame, or at least handleable, it is *not* domestic. The fact that it is a wild animal, and a pretty sizable one at that, is part of the iguana's allure. But also be aware that iguanas will become defensive and sometimes actually aggressive, if teased. By treating your captive properly you reinforce nonaggressive behavior.

Before we learned the mechanics of keeping iguanas alive for extended periods, the subject of breeding season aggression was seldom raised. Thankfully for the iguanas, this is no longer the case. We can and do keep them alive, and more and more of these big lizards are reaching the size and age where hormonally induced lizard-keeper confrontations occur. You must now confront the possibility that sometime you will be bitten by your "tame" iguana. And the bite will probably come when, unless you're adept at reading iguana body language, you simply don't expect it. Although a bite from an iguana may be little more than a casual nip, a deliberate, aggressive bite will at the very least require a visit to your local hospital emergency room and antibiotics. (Hand wounds are rarely stitched to avoid abesses.) At the very least, you should always have your tetanus shots up to date.

Here are some facts to be aware of pertaining to breeding iguanas:

1. When properly cared for, great green iguanas become sexually mature at from one and a half to three years of age. At that time, their size may vary from 28 inches to 40 inches (71–102 cm) in length.

2. A great green iguana female does not require the presence of a male or the act of being bred to lay eggs. Ovulation and subsequent egg production can occur even when a single female is being kept. The demands on the reserves of females, including calcium usage, seem the same whether the eggs are fertile or not.

3. There is some indication that infertile eggs may be more difficult

Male green iguanas in the wild collect harems of female iguanas, all of whom are free to wander out of the male's range any time they wish. In captivity, this young male iguana can only select a display perch and hope a female will wander by.

for a female to lay than fertile eggs; this seemed particularly so with very young females laying their first clutch. But infertile eggs are not the only reason for a female's difficulty in laying. A broken or malformed egg, overly large clutches, improper hydration, improper calcium levels, and an unsatisfactory deposition site can also lead to egg retention. There is no surefire method to assure that egg binding does not occur, but here are a few actions the hobbyist can take to lessen the chances of this occurring:

• Make certain that your gravid female iguana is eating plenty of moist vegetables and always has clean water available. Proper hydration is *very* important!

• Make certain your gravid female iguana is receiving ample calcium in her diet. Laying down the shell, as the process is called, takes a lot of calcium. If the female doesn't have enough calcium available, calcium will be taken from her bones for the eggshells.

• Make certain that your female iguana has a satisfactory egg-laying site available both day and night.

• Egg binding can result in ruptured oviducts and if untreated, the ultimate death of your iguana. Veterinary intervention is mandatory.

4. Although both male and female great green iguanas may become aggressive, and may do so at any time of their lives, it is the sexually active males that are most apt to become problematic. Simply put, male green iguanas want sex, plain and simple. Aggression and dominance is a way of life for sexually active male iguanas of all species, and for most lizards in general.

While young, neither male nor female iguanas get stressed out by seasonal hormonal changes.

5. In an effort to assure the continuation of their genetic lineage, during the lengthy breeding season, male iguanas display, bluff, bluster, and, if need be, actually fight adversaries. There are times when your testosterone-driven male iguana may view you as an adversary and there are often certain things—a particular motion perceived by the lizard as being submissive, a particular color, or even the pheromones of a female keeper—that may trigger aggressive overtures.

6. Reproductive readiness is usually triggered, at least in part, by increasing photoperiods. Denying your iguana more than ten hours of illumination a day may forestall breeding displays.

7. It is important that you learn, and heed, iguana body language.

When the iguana is alert, each movement has a meaning, at least to iguanas, and should to you. What starts with bluff can turn to aggression, but if you're alert, you can outbluff your iguana.

Signs of Reproductive Readiness

If your iguana's body color brightens or shifts from a healthy green to a brighter green or to hues of orange, it is very likely that it is beginning what can be a lengthy period of reproductive readiness. There are other signs as well:

• Sitting alertly, anterior body lifted high on extended forelimbs. This

When Can Your Iguanas Breed?

It seems that size, rather than age, determines a great green iguana's ability to breed. When growth rate is "normal," research has determined that a female green iguana may ovulate anytime after she has attained 10 inches (25 cm) in snout-vent length. A male can breed anytime after reaching 6 inches (15 cm) in snout-vent length. A female iguana growing at a normal rate, therefore, can ovulate anytime after she is about 15 months of age, and the male can breed a month or two sooner.

You have coped successfully with the day-to-day challenges posed by your green iguana, and have watched the lizard grow from the tiny, 10-inch-long (25 cm) hatchling it was when you became beguiled with it at the pet store, to a robust, two-year-old, 36-inch-long (91 cm), subadult lizard that just happens to be a female. Suddenly, before your very eyes, she begins to gain weight, but is at the same time seemingly eating less. A month and a half later, her once sleek body lines are pudgy and showing the contours of rounded eggs within.

It is believed that ovulation by the females of some lizard species (anoles) is stimulated by viewing the display sequence of a male. Even this formality is not necessary with the great green iguana. A female iguana may ovulate and produce eggs even when a male is neither present nor visible. Spontaneous ovulation and development of infertile eggs is a common event. Early spaying can prevent all of the possible problems listed on page 134.

often precedes the beginning of territoriality display and is a good time to outbluff your iguana.
• Body laterally compressed to make a male look larger. This is the beginning of territoriality display. Terminate this promptly.
• Dewlap fully extended, nuchal (neck) crest pulled erect by muscle contraction, head moving in short, abrupt, vertical nods. This is the next step of territoriality display; do not ignore.
• Anterior body—sometimes the whole body—pushups, often rather rapid. There's still time to back him down.

• Approaching ("sidling huffily") with his body lateral to you. Watch the tail and teeth; back him down, *now!*

Warning: There may be times when all of the above are dispensed with, and your iguana responds to your presence with a fast dash forward with intent to deliver a tearing bite. This can be hard to avoid. Loose floor-length clothing may take the bite intended for you. Be alert!

How to Back Down an Aggressive Iguana
• Cage your iguana during the breeding season, but be aware that

In Miami, green iguanas will wander widely in search of the best food, the best place to swim, and the best selection of females. (No parallel with humans is intended.)

at this time normally quiet iguanas may injure themselves by trying continually to escape. Be observant and ready to modify your method of control if necessary.

• Surgical castration may help (see page 139).

• Keep UVA and UVB availability to no more than ten hours a day.

• Before the display becomes too tense, you may be able to simply lift your iguana and pet him, thereby gently reasserting your dominance. But be careful! Hormones are at work and this may not work. Your iguana may try hard to bite.

• You can bluff your iguana by taking the aggressive path. Taking a cue from the displaying lizard, make *yourself* look as large and aggressive as possible. Respond *"No"* in a loud voice; extend your arms to your side making yourself look as big as possible, show no sign of flinching,

and stride determinedly toward the lizard.

• Respected iguana keeper Melissa Kaplan suggests allowing a male iguana access to a soft towel or stuffed sock on which to vent its sexual frustrations.

Nests and Nesting

During the periods of reduced light, temperature, humidity, and rainfall, reduction by the iguana in the production of certain key hormones causes ovarian and testicular regression. With the lengthening days and correspondingly increasing warmth, humidity, and rain activity of spring and summer, hormonal production again increases, causing the changes that stimulate interest in reproduction. With the increase in the production of testosterone also comes increased interest in territoriality with a correspondingly increased aggressive attitude toward rival males and, sometimes, toward keepers. It is at this time that what may have until then been compatible groups of iguanas are apt to become quarrelsome.

Nesting Preparations

Female iguanas put their all into nesting preparations. After choosing a suitable site, they will dig deeply into the earth with their forefeet. Loosened dirt and debris are removed with the rear feet. When finished, the hole will be sufficiently large for the female to completely seclude herself in it while laying. She prefers a cozy excavation, one where her head hits the top of the hole. Usually, several times during preparations, the female will reverse her head-down position and peer from the deepening chamber, perhaps scouting for approaching danger. Certainly at this time, while head-down in a constraining hole, an adult female iguana is more vulnerable to predation than at almost any other time in her life.

The nesting efforts may be curtailed at any time during the preparation. If disturbed by a predator, or if the digging is thwarted by a maze of roots or rocks, the female will often leave to begin again elsewhere at another time. Even if completed after several periods of digging interspersed with periods of rest, the female, based upon criteria known best to her, may deem the nesting

Male iguanas can breed when they reach a snout-vent length of 6 inches, or about 18 inches overall.

chamber unsuitable. Should this be the case, the female will abandon the completed but unused nest and proceed at another location.

If all seems well with the initial excavation, the female will, after a period of rest, lay and position each egg of her clutch, then fill the hole with the removed dirt, and leave. Female Allen's Cay iguanas do not leave their nests, but defend the site from other females who might tear up the nest with their digging. Depending on temperature and moisture, the period of incubation can and will vary considerably. At the low end, under ideal nest conditions, the eggs may hatch in about

Iguanas can be quite individualistic in their behavior during breeding season. Simon, despite his appearance, was never aggressive toward his owners.

Outdoor Iguanas

Iguanas kept out-of-doors in the southernmost areas of our country can be allowed to breed and nest nearly as they would in the wild. We, as owners, merely need to ascertain that suitable nesting areas are present in the cages. There are a few cues that your female is ready to lay. She generally looks fat, with her belly distended by the eggs. She will become crabby one to two weeks before egg deposition and become anorexic as well. If a gravid female iguana does not initially begin her own nest, and you feel the substrate is suitable, merely disturbing the surface of the ground may be an adequate prompt. Occasionally, a female can be induced to nest naturally by providing her with a secluded area, such as the bottom third of a large, dark-colored, plastic trash can with an entry hole cut in it, inverted over the most suitable spot, within which she may dig. In other cases, where caging conditions are less natural, a suitable nesting chamber must be constructed for the female iguana.

Several nest models seem equally well accepted by gravid female iguanas. Suitability seems governed by certain considerations, such as adequate (but not big) amounts of space and darkness as well as appropriate moisture content and temperature.

In-ground Nests

An in-ground nest can easily be made in one of two ways: by digging down and framing an adequately

70 days. Under cooler, drier conditions the incubation duration may near 139 days; in the wild, the average is 90 days.

Tame, content, and healthy iguanas make the best breeders. If your iguanas are fearful and skittish, breeding sequences are easily interrupted. It may take your female some time to become accustomed to the nesting chamber prior to egg deposition, especially with artificial chambers. Be ready however; have your incubator on and calibrated.

sized depression with wood, or by sinking the inverted bottom third of a large, dark-colored (dark brown or black), heavy plastic trash can in the ground. In either case, an entryway must be left open. It will be necessary to cover the wooden chamber with a piece of plywood or other suitably opaque top. The gravid female iguana may either deposit her eggs right in this chamber as provided, or she may scratch an additional depression in the dirt that the chamber covers. Although many breeders feel that iguanas favor rather long entranceways to their artificial in-ground nesting chambers, these are certainly not mandatory. However, should you decide to provide one, it is easily made by laying one or more lengths of ceramic pipe of suitable diameter on their side—end to end if more than a single piece is used—sloping them downward from the ground surface to the entrance of the main nesting chamber.

Above-ground Nests

An above-ground nest can easily be made by using a large, dark-colored, rigid plastic trash can. A can with four flat sides is the easiest to work with.

1. Choose an area of the pen where the can will not overheat.

2. Cut an entrance hole in an upper corner of the top.

3. Securely affix the top to the bottom.

4. Lay the can on one of its broad sides.

5. Fill the entire length of the horizontal can half to three-quarters full with a barely moistened mixture of half sand/half soil. A little peat can be mixed in to help retain moisture and lighten the mixture somewhat.

6. If the moisture, temperature, and soil consistency are suitable, the female iguana will dig her burrow and nesting chamber, and deposit her eggs. This trash can arrangement may also be used successfully in indoor settings.

Eggs

Green iguanas may lay from 10 to 70 (rarely even more) eggs. An average clutch from a healthy adult female numbers between 35 and 45 eggs. The large clutches of relatively small eggs are evidently an adaptation to an environment of seasonally abundant food and heavy predation. A large number of physically less-developed babies are hatched. In contrast, insular populations of other iguanas have fewer predators but more restricted food resources, and these iguanids lay smaller clutches of larger eggs.

Despite what many people may think, life in the tropics is seasonal. There are distinct and regular dry seasons, and high-quality food plants are intermittently available. The breeding cycle of iguanas is based on these factors. During the dry season, winds blow and males display longer in their sunlit, exposed perches. Iguana eggs are laid at the beginning of the dry season, when the soil heats up enough to serve as an incubator. The young iguanas emerge at the beginning of the rainy season, just as new leaves appear on the plants, and daily rains soften the soil and make digging out less work.

Green iguana eggs are laid about 70 to 85 days following copulation. The eggs have a pliable and permeable parchmentlike shell. If the female iguana is properly hydrated, the eggs will be semiturgid when laid.

Their permeable eggshells allow the eggs to desiccate or overhydrate by losing moisture to, or absorbing moisture from, the substrate. They will gain weight for the first 60 to 84 days of incubation. Watch the eggs closely during incubation. If the eggs begin to collapse, increase the moisture *slightly*; if they get turgid and slick, decrease the moisture. Do note, however, that even under ideal incubation conditions, when full term is neared, dimpling and a concurrent lack of eggshell turgidity is normal.

At a temperature of 85 to 87°F (29.4–31°C), incubation takes from 60 to nearly 90 days. Babies stay in the egg until the yolk is absorbed, and will emerge at the same time. If your incubation temperatures are too high, your babies may emerge with smaller than normal eyes, bad vision, and scoliosis.

Dystocia

It has been well documented that very young female lizards producing their first clutch of eggs may suffer from dystocia (egg retention). This is especially true if the eggs are infertile. There seems to be a tendency for this problem to occur in green iguanas. Let there be no mistake, dystocia can be fatal, even when veterinary intervention is sought.

Contributing Causes of Dystocia

• Ovulation and egg formation at too young an age.
• Insufficient hydration of the female.
• Insufficient exercise space for the female.
• Improper or unsatisfactory deposition site provided.
• Improperly formed eggs (adherent, abnormally shaped or sized, improperly calcified eggshells).
• Overly large clutch.

Although it is best if your iguana is at least two and a half years of age—three and a half is probably even better—there is really very little you can do to control the age at which she (spontaneously) ovulates.

You must hope that Mother Nature is looking after some of the potential egg-laying problems that your iguana may experience, but you can certainly give her an assist on some aspects.

As growing eggs take up ever more of the space in your female iguana's body cavity, she will eat less. Since a good portion of her moisture requirements are derived from her food, less food intake may mean a moisture deficit.

Female iguanas may have difficulty in laying their first clutch of eggs. Make certain her supplements are adequate.

• Be sure that she always has plenty of clean drinking water readily available.

• Be absolutely sure that the quarters of your female iguana are brilliantly illuminated by full-spectrum bulbs or that she gets some unfiltered sunshine daily.

• Be sure she has room to walk and climb as she chooses.

• Provide some D_3 and calcium as dietary additives (see page 101).

• Provide a suitable nesting box.

If, even after you have done everything possible to assure proper egg laying, your female iguana does not lay (full gestation is about 55 to 60 days), you must consider dystocia.

Sadly, improper egg shapes, shell calcification, adhesion (to other eggs or to the walls of the oviduct), or overly large clutches are not at all uncommon. All of these will require veterinary intervention to correct.

Dystocia can be divided into two categories: preovulatory retention and postovulatory retention. Blood analyses, plasma biochemistries, and radiographs may be required to determine the scope of the problem.

Preovulatory retention is often accompanied by elevated phosphorus and calcium levels, and eventually by renal failure. Various stages of metabolic bone disease may also be detected. Stabilization and spaying—a bilateral ovariosalpingectomy—will be required but may not save the iguana.

Postovulatory retention is accompanied by listlessness, cumbersome movements, and acute dehydration. Stabilization followed by surgery is the treatment of choice here. If treated soon enough the prognosis for the iguana is usually good.

Note: Find a reptile-oriented veterinarian before an emergency strikes.

Incubation

Removing the Eggs

Following deposition, remove the eggs as soon as possible for incubation. It seems best, but may not be as critical as we once thought, if the orientation in which the egg was found is not changed. In other words, just to be safe, keep the same side up. Unlike a bird's eggs, most of which are regularly turned by the setting female, once laid, a reptile's eggs are not turned during incubation.

The medium: The chosen incubation medium—Perlite, vermiculite, or sphagnum moss are all fine—should be moistened. One and a quarter cup to one-half cup of water is a start; you want damp medium that you can't squeeze any water out of when you clench some in your fist. The end result should be that the medium is moist but not wet. Place an inch or inch and a half (2.5–3.8 cm) of the medium in the bottom of a nonventilated plastic box. The eggs of iguanas should be at least one-half to two-thirds buried in the substrate. Once the eggs are in place, put the lid on the box and place in the incubator. If you have accurate scales, weigh the box and eggs so you can later determine any evaporation from the medium. A shallow open dish of water in the incubator will help keep the relative humidity high.

Sex determination: Although the sex of some lizard species is determined by the temperature at which the egg is incubated—temperature-dependent sex determination—this does not seem to be so with iguanas. Both males and females are produced at all suitable incubation temperatures—genetically determined sex. **To repeat:** The preferred incubation temperatures are between 85 and 87°F (29.4–31°C) and hatching will occur after 60 to 90 days of incubation.

Making Your Own Incubator

Materials needed for one incubator:

• 1 wafer thermostat/heater, obtainable from feed stores; these are commonly used in incubators for chicks
• 1 thermometer
• 1 Styrofoam cooler, with thick sides; a fish shipping box is ideal
• 1 heat tape
• 1 electrical cord and wall plug
• 3 wire nuts
• a piece of heavy wire mesh, large enough to bend into a U-shaped shelf.

Your goal is to wire the thermostat into the circuitry between the heat-emitting tape and the electrical cord, to allow you to regulate the temperature of your incubator.

1. Cut the electric cord section about in half; in all cases leave at least 18 inches (46 cm) of electrical cord attached to the heat tape.

2. Poke a hole through the side of the Styrofoam cooler about 5 inches (13 cm) below the top.

3. Pull the non-heat-taped section of the electric cord through the hole, keeping the plug on the outside.

Don't plug it in until all modifications are finished.

4. Remove a half inch (13 mm) of insulation from the cut ends of both sections of the electrical cord and separate each of the two wires for a few inches.

5. Carefully following the directions that come with the wafer thermostat, and using a wire nut, connect one of the wire leads extending from the heat tape to the designated red wire from the thermostat. Use the second wire nut to connect the second of the thermostat's red wires to one lead from the plug-in section. The third wire nut will connect the remaining unattached lead from the plug-in section to the still unattached lead from the heat tape.

6. Poke a small hole through the lid of the Styro cooler, and suspend the thermostat/heater from the inside.

7. Add another hole for a thermometer, so you can check on the inside temperature without opening the top. If there's no flange on the thermometer to keep it from slipping through the hole in the lid, use a rubber band wound several times around the thermometer to form a flange. Place the heat tape in a loose coil on the bottom.

8. Put the lid on the Styro cooler, and plug in the thermostat/heater. Wait half an hour and check the temperature. Adjust the thermostat/heater until the temperature inside the incubator is about 86°F (30°C).

The L-pin "handle" on the top of the thermostat is the rheostat.

9. Once you have the temperature regulated, put the container of eggs inside the incubator and close the lid.

Check the temperature daily. Weigh the egg box to determine if any water has evaporated from the incubating medium. Add a little water to the incubating medium as needed. The preferred humidity is 100 percent, which can be accomplished by keeping the hatching medium of peat and soil damp to the touch but too dry to squeeze out any water when squeezed by your hand.

How do you know if the eggs are fertile or viable? Soon, following laying, those eggs that are not fertile will turn yellow, harden, and begin to collapse. Should embryo death occur during incubation, discoloration often soon follows. Fertile eggs will remain white and turgid to the touch. Infertile eggs should be removed and discarded.

Evidently undistressed by facial wounds received in a tussle with another male, a male green iguana seems to relish a meal of fresh greens. The wounds proved to be superficial.

At the end of the incubation period, which may vary in duration from 60 to 80 days, the baby iguanas will pip. The babies may remain in the pipped egg for as long as a day and a half. Once they have hatched, they should be moved to another terrarium and offered food, a sunning spot, and water.

Aggressive Nature

There is one fact about great green iguanas that you will soon experience firsthand: If they are properly cared for, they grow—and they grow and they grow. Females often attain a length of more that 3½ feet (104 cm), and occasionally may attain 4½ feet (135 cm). Males often attain 5½ to 6 feet (165–183 cm), and occasionally exceed 6½ feet (196 cm) by an inch or two (2.5–5 cm).

By any standards, iguanas are big lizards. And no matter how much you like iguanas, and how often you handle them, or how long you've had them, or how tame they've been while growing, once they have attained sexual maturity, not all iguanas (especially males) remain tractable.

Male iguanas especially display unpredictable behavior during the breeding season and may become especially aggressive toward a female owner. The need for careful approach and handling cannot be overemphasized

A severe bite by a 6-foot-long (1.8 m), up to 18-pound (8.2 kg), testosterone-driven male iguana on a hand, finger, or face can be bloody and painful at best, and can require reconstructive surgery at worst. Because of the temperament and size differences, the bite by an adult female may not be nearly as bad, but this can be a moot point. The jaws of these lizards are immensely powerful and both jaws are liberally studded with sharp teeth. The teeth can make minced meat out of anything they bite.

Danger Signs

What are the danger signs? They can be pretty small, but they add up. Your iguana can smell, and males as well as females are aware of the monthly cycles of females of other species; males seem more hostile when their female owner is in her menstrual cycle.

Your iguana's behavior will alter when you're near. It may watch you more alertly and raise the forepart of its body as you approach. Males may darken slightly in color, and the dewlap and spinal crest are displayed.

Neutering

Can you avoid this sort of problem? Yes, to a degree; remember, these are wild animals we are talking about, not a reptilian pet that's been domesticated for 100 years. For many iguana owners, the answer is neutering.

The neutering of an iguana is a fairly controversial subject. The procedure is so new with iguanas, that the benefits, real or imagined, are still being assessed. Additionally, not all veterinarians feel qualified, or inclined, to perform the surgery. However, for males, castration actually helps to modify the behavior of these testosterone-stimulated lizards.

When to Neuter

Castration should be considered by iguana owners who do not wish to breed their lizards, or who are unable to contend with the hormonally induced mood swings of a sexually mature adult. Because males are larger and stronger, their sudden and unexpected bouts of aggression toward their owner can be particularly unnerving and have potential for serious damage. If you are considering this surgery, please note that surgery seems most successful in circumventing moodiness and aggres-

sion when performed before the iguana reaches sexual maturity. If an adult male iguana is castrated at the height of his period of reproductive aggressiveness, his disposition may change little, or not at all.

Sexual maturity may be earlier than you might think. The iguana species, like all animals, depends on having a certain number of their young reach sexual maturity and live long enough to reproduce. One way is to produce lots of babies. With egg clutches of 30 plus eggs once a year, and a productive life span of 10 to 15 years, iguanas can do this. Another way is to start early. Female iguanas can ovulate at a body length of 10 inches (25 cm), and males are sexually reproductive at a body length of 6 inches (15 cm). In other words, an iguana of less than one year of age can reproduce. It is not unusual for females, especially young females, to produce infertile egg masses with no male in sight or within smelling distance. The egg masses may not fully shell or be passable by the female, requiring surgical removal/intervention. Compared to this, spaying sounds like a very reasonable alternative.

Spaying or castration is not inexpensive, it is not entirely risk-free, nor is it a fool-proof cure for aggressiveness, but it should be considered a viable option for iguana keepers who wish to keep their female iguanas healthy, and to reduce the possibility of sustaining an iguana bite. Surgical castration is an option worth discussing with your reptile veterinarian.

Appendix
Photographing Iguanas

Within the United States, you can seek out iguanas for field observations and photographic purposes without concerning yourself about permits.

To observe Florida's and Texas' green and spiny-tailed iguanas, you will need patience and binoculars, and should you choose to photograph them, you will need luck and a good telephoto lens. Feral iguanas can be as difficult to approach as the wildest bird.

Iguanas are often most easily observed in public gardens, parks, and other such well-vegetated areas. They are also frequently encountered along drainage canals in urban and suburban settings. Look for iguanas near culverts, on rock piles, or suitable elevated basking perches. In Miami and Homestead, Florida, the big lizards may often be seen along the banks of canals, sprawled over several branches of the introduced pest-shrub referred to as Florida holly or Brazilian pepper. Introduced iguanas are abundant on Virginia Key, Key Biscayne, and near Miami International Airport. They also occur in and near Brownsville, Texas.

Green iguanas are most readily sighted during the breeding season when they are a little bolder and often much more brightly colored than usual. Bright orange males can be seen for several blocks as they sun and display from the tops of fences, walls, and thickets. The males expand their dewlaps, raise their heads haughtily, and all but shout "Baby, get a load of this!" Gravid females may be found constructing nests, often near human-generated debris, along canal banks.

To see and photograph desert iguana, go to the deserts of western Arizona, eastern California, and southern Nevada. These lizards may be seen crossing the desert roadways and foraging near creosote brush over much of that region. Chuckwallas occur in the same geographic area as the desert iguana but are restricted to boulder fields and similar habitats.

Equipment Needed

The equipment required for photographing lizards will depend upon

a number of variables. Among these are whether you will be taking photos of large lizards or small lizards, whether they will be captive, staged, or in the wild, and whether you are willing to devote to the hobby the time necessary to be successful. Of course, photographing captive or staged lizards is infinitely easier than pursuing and photographing free-ranging ones, but not nearly as satisfying.

Technique

Approach the iguana you hope to photograph slowly and obliquely. Avoid eye contact. We begin taking pictures when we are still much too far away, but feel that a record of an iguana so distant that identification is still tenuous is better than no photo at all, and some iguanas sim-

ply are too wary to allow close approach.

Iguanas of many species may also be photographed at zoological parks. In indoor situations a flash will invariably be necessary. To avoid reflection, position your flash unit at an angle to the glass front of the cage. To compensate for the thickness of the glass, it is usually necessary to open your lens at least one *f*-stop wider than indicated by your meter.

We used film cameras for years, but digital photography offers many advantages over film. We prefer Canon SLR cameras with with additional wide-angle and macro lenses, but there are many good brands to select from. Be certain the camera you buy can take distance, nearby, and close-up photos. A tripod may be a useful addition.

Glossary

Aestivation: A period of warm weather inactivity; often triggered by excessive heat or drought.

Albino: Lacking black pigment.

Ambient temperature: The temperature of the surrounding environment.

Anterior: Toward the front.

Anus: The external opening of the cloaca; the vent.

Arboreal: Tree-dwelling.

Attenuated: Long and slender, as a green iguana's original tail.

Brumation: The reptilian and amphibian equivalent of mammalian hibernation.

Caudal: Pertaining to the tail.

cb/cb: Captive-bred, captive-born.

cb/ch: Captive-bred, captive-hatched.

Chorioallantois: The gas-permeable membranous layer inside the shell of a reptile egg.

Clade: A grouping of closely aligned reptiles, all in the same species but as yet not placed into subspecies designations

Cloaca: The common chamber into which digestive, urinary, and reproductive systems empty and that itself opens exteriorly through the vent or anus.

Crepuscular: Active at dusk and/or dawn.

Crest: A ridge, usually of enlarged or attenuated scales along the nape, back, and/or basal tail area of an iguana.

Deposition: As used here, the laying of the eggs or birthing of young.

Deposition site: The spot chosen by the female to lay her eggs or have young.

Dimorphic: A difference in form, build, or coloration involving the same species; often sex-linked.

Display: The act of body inflation, crest erection, huffing, mouth feints, and color changes used by male and female iguanas to defend territory (males) or nesting sites (females).

Diurnal: Active in the daytime.

Dorsal: Pertaining to the back; upper surface.

Dorsolateral: Pertaining to the upper sides.

Dorsum: The upper surface.

Dystocia: Difficulty in laying eggs or giving birth.

Ecological niche: The precise habitat utilized by a species.

Ectothermic: Cold-blooded.

Electrophoresis: The movement of suspended particles through a fluid subjected to an electrical charge;

used to quantify genetic differences in species populations.

Endemic: Confined to a specific region.

Endothermic: Warm-blooded.

Femoral pores: Openings on the underside of the thighs of a lizard; the pores produce a waxy exudate that creates a scent trail.

Femur: The part of the leg between the knee and the hip.

Form: An identifiable species or subspecies.

Fracture planes: Soft areas in the caudal vertebrae that break easily, allowing the tail to be pulled free from the lizard's body.

Genus: A taxonomic classification of a group of species having similar characteristics. The genus falls between the next higher designation of "family" and the next lower designation of "species." It is always capitalized when written. Genera is the plural of genus.

Glottis: The opening of the windpipe.

Granular: Pertaining to small, flat scales.

Gravid: The reptilian equivalent of mammalian pregnancy.

Gular: Pertaining to the throat.

Hatchling: An iguana (in this case) newly emerged from the egg.

Heliothermic: Pertaining to a species that basks in the sun to thermoregulate.

Hemipenes: The dual copulatory organs of male lizards.

Hemipenis: The singular form of hemipenes.

Herpetoculture: The captive breeding of reptiles and amphibians.

Herpetoculturist: One who indulges in herpetoculture.

Herpetologist: One who indulges in herpetology.

Herpetology: The study (often scientifically oriented) of reptiles and amphibians.

Hibernacula: Winter dens.

Hybrid: Offspring from the breeding of two species.

Hydrate: To restore body moisture by drinking or absorption.

Jacobson's organs: Highly enervated olfactory pits in the palate of lizards.

Juvenile: A young or immature specimen.

Labial: Pertaining to the lips.

Lateral: Pertaining to the side.

Melanism: A profusion of black pigment.

Middorsal: Pertaining to the middle of the back.

Midventral: Pertaining to the center of the belly or abdomen.

Monotypic: Containing but one type.

Nocturnal: Active at night.

Ocelli: Dots or "eye spots," often with a lighter center, on a lizard's skin.

Oviparous: Reproducing by means of eggs that hatch after laying.

Parietal eye: A sensory organ positioned midcranially in certain lizards.

Phalanges: Bones of the toes.

Photoperiod: The daily/seasonally variable length of the hours of daylight.

Poikilothermic: A species with no internal body temperature regulation. The old term was cold-blooded. Ectothermic.

Postocular: To the rear of the eye.

Premaxillary: Bones at the front of the upper jaw.

Saxicolous: Rock-dwelling.

Scute: Scale.

SNV: Snout-vent length, or the body length of the iguana. This serves as a useful comparison in overall size for a lizard whose overall length depends on whether its tail has been broken or not.

Species: A group of similar creatures that produce viable young when bred together; the taxonomic designation that falls beneath genus and above subspecies. Abbreviation: "sp."

Subspecies: The subdivision of a species, differing in range, colors, size, scalation, or other criteria.

Taxonomy: The science of classification of plants and animals.

Terrestrial: Land-dwelling.

Thermoreceptive: Sensitive to heat.

Thermoregulate: To regulate (body) temperature by choosing a warmer or cooler environment.

Thigmothermic: Pertaining to a species, often nocturnal, that thermoregulates by being in contact with a preheated surface such as a boulder or tarred road surface.

Tubercles: Warty protuberances.

Tympanum: The external eardrum.

Vent: The external opening of the cloaca; the anus.

Venter: The underside of a creature; the belly.

Ventral: Pertaining to the undersurface or belly.

Ventrolateral: Pertaining to the sides of the venter (belly).

Vestigial: Degenerated.

Note: Other scientific definitions are contained in the following two volumes:

Peters, James A. *Dictionary of Herpetology.* New York: Hafner Publishing Co., 1964.

Wareham, David C. *The Reptile and Amphibian Keeper's Dictionary.* London: Blandford, 1993.

Useful Addresses and Literature

Organizations

The International Iguana Society
Route 3, Box 328
Big Pine Key, FL 33043

The International Iguana Society is a nonprofit corporation dedicated to the conservation, biological diversity, and secondarily, the herpetoculture of the iguanas of the world. Recognizing that many taxa are in immediate jeopardy, the IIS assists the appropriate governments and governmental agencies establish guidelines to assure the continued existence of all iguanid lizards. Although the main thrust of the IIS is oriented toward the vari-ous West Indian rock iguanas of the genus *Cyclura*, problems concerning all iguanid taxa are recognized and considered. A quarterly newsletter, the *Iguana Times*, is sent to members.

Utila Iguana Conservation Project
c/o Dr. Gunther Koehler
Senckenberg Museum
Sektion Herpetologie
Senckenberganlage 25
D-60325 Frankfurt a.M.
Germany

The Utila iguana is one of the insular iguanas in danger from over-hunting habitat destruction. Once

Web Sites

These web sites were current at the time of publication of this book. If your connection is lost, or if your server cannot find the address, try a search for the site name.

Henry Lizardlover	herp.com/henry/
Iguana Den	escape.com/~iggyden
Giant Green Iguana Care	sonic.net/~melissk.ig-care.html
Wog's Green Iguana Page	mail.milagros.net/caiman

found on the Utila, Bonacca, and Roatan islands in Honduras, the iguana is now endemic to Utila. The conservation project sponsors local education programs and *in situ* breeding programs. Mangrove and swamp destruction on the island of Utila has placed this species at grave risk.

Pro Iguana Verde Foundation
c/o Dr. Dagmar Werner
Apartado 692-1007
San José
Costa Rica

The Pro Iguana Verde Foundation takes the concept of sustainable development back to the jungle. The foundation seeks to preserve Costa Rica's forest and provide local income by managing buffer zones to increase habitat and the fauna populations. Farmers become self-sufficient without destroying their environment. They raise, release, and hunt iguanas, and produce iguana leather products and handicrafts. During the first five years of operation, 80,000 green iguanas were raised and released into the forest. Iguana Park is licensed to sell iguana meat and iguana products.

Societies and Magazines

Herpetological societies exist in many larger cities. Very experienced herpetoculturists are often among their ranks. These societies are excellent sources of information and camaraderie for both the new iguana keeper and those with more expertise. The existence of a herpetological society can often be ascertained by checking with pet shop employees, local museums, or zoos. Periodically updated listings of existing societies are often included as a public service by the several national magazines dedicated to the field of herpetology and herpetoculture. Among others occasionally available, the following magazines are available either through subscription, pet shops, or on newsstands.

Reptiles
P.O. Box 6050
Mission Viejo, CA 92690-6050

The Vivarium
AFH
P.O. Box 300067
Escondido, CA 92030-0067

Copeia
ASIH
Department of Zoology
Southern Illinois University
Carbondale, IL 62901-6501

Herp Review and *The Journal of Herpetology*
SSRA
Department of Zoology
Miami University
Oxford, OH 45056

Other References

Burghardt, G. M. and A. S. Rand, eds. *Iguanas of the World: Their Behavior, Ecology and Conservation.* Park Ridge, NJ. Noyes Publishing, 1983.

Donoghue, Susan. "Growth of Juvenile Green Iguanas Fed Four Diets." *Journal of Nutrition* 124, 2626S-2629S, 1994.

Jacobson, Elliott, editor. *Biology, Husbandry and Medicine of the Green Iguana*. Malabar, FL. Krieger Publishing, 2008.

Index